Brilliant
Mac Basics

Second edition
Joli Ballew

PEARSON

Harlow, England • London • New York • Boston • San Francisco • Toronto • Sydney • Auckland • Singapore • Hong Kong
Tokyo • Seoul • Taipei • New Delhi • Cape Town • São Paulo • Mexico City • Madrid • Amsterdam • Munich • Paris • Milan

Pearson Education Limited
Edinburgh Gate
Harlow CM20 2JE
United Kingdom
Tel: +44 (0)1279 623623
Fax: +44 (0)1279 431059
Website: www.pearsoned.co.uk

First edition 2008
Second edition 2012

Pearson Education is not responsible for the content of third party Internet sites.

ISBN: 978-0-273-76507-3

British Library Cataloguing-in-Publication Data
A catalogue record for this book is available from the British Library

Library of Congress Cataloging-in-Publication Data
A catalogue record for this book is avaliable from the British Library

10 9 8 7 6 5 4 3 2 1
15 14 13 12 11

Typeset in 11pt Arial Condensed by 30
Printed in Great Britain by Scotprint, Haddington.

Brilliant guides

What you need to know and how to do it

When you're working on your computer and come up against a problem that you're unsure how to solve, or want to accomplish something in an application that you aren't sure how to do, where do you look? Manuals and traditional training guides are usually too big and unwieldy and are intended to be used as end-to-end training resources, making it hard to get to the info you need right away without having to wade through pages of background information that you just don't need at that moment – and helplines are rarely that helpful!

Brilliant guides have been developed to allow you to find the info you need easily and without fuss and guide you through the task using a highly visual, step-by-step approach – providing exactly what you need to know when you need it!

Brilliant guides provide the quick easy-to-access information that you need, using a table of contents and troubleshooting guide to help you find exactly what you need to know, and then presenting each task in a visual manner. Numbered steps guide you through each task or problem, using numerous screenshots to illustrate each step. Added features include 'See also...' boxes that point you to related tasks and information in the book, while 'Did you know?...' sections alert you to relevant expert tips, tricks and advice to further expand your skills and knowledge.

In addition to covering all major office PC applications, and related computing subjects, the *Brilliant* series also contains titles that will help you in every aspect of your working life, such as writing the perfect CV, answering the toughest interview questions and moving on in your career.

Brilliant guides are the light at the end of the tunnel when you are faced with any minor or major task.

Author's acknowledgements

Pearson and I go way back. I'm starting to feel like part of a family. If I'm not mistaken, this is our 14th or 15th book together in less than six years, and I am very proud of the relationships we have fostered during that time. It's been an amazing run with lots of opportunities and successes for us all.

I would like to thank Steve Temblett, Robert Cottee, Katy Robinson and Helen Savill for guiding me through this book. They are all thoughtful, kind and great leaders, and let me do just about anything I want to do and in almost any time frame. I couldn't ask for any better publishing team.

As my faithful readers know, I have a family to thank, too. I have my Dad, Cosmo, Jennifer and Andrew, and a few others who are related in various ways through them. My mom passed away in February of 2009 and, while expected, it hit me harder than I thought it would. Everyone recovers from such tragedies, though, and generally we end up stronger for it in the end. I can say that's true for me, as I have grown intellectually and spiritually, and am faster to forgive and slower to anger. Mom would be proud. I wish she were here to see how I've grown and how well I'm taking care of Dad (who turned 90 in 2010).

I am also thankful for Neil Salkind Ph.D. of the Salkind Literary Agency. He is my agent, but he is also my friend and mentor. He and his team read my contracts and manage my minor disputes and complaints, they watch my royalty statements and payments, and Neil secures books deals and does all of the other things you'd expect from an agent, but he's much more than that: he's a friend, too. We celebrated ten years together in 2011, during which we've published 40 or so books. That's a long time in agent–writer years.

Finally, thanks to you, my most awesome readers and fans. May you find this book helpful and easy to understand, and I sincerely hope it assists you in getting the very most out of your Mac computer. My door is an open one. Feel free to contact me any time at joli_ballew@hotmail.com, and be assured I'll write back. I love to hear from my readers.

Publisher's acknowledgements

Brilliant Mac Basics, 2nd edition draws on the research and writings of Jerry Glenwright, as published in *Brilliant Mac Basics*, 1st edition.

About the author

Joli Ballew (Dallas, Texas) is a technical author, a technology trainer and website manager, and has published more than 40 books which have been translated into ten languages. She holds several certifications, including MCSE, MCTS and MCDST. Joli is also a Microsoft MVP (four years running), and attends the Microsoft Summit as well as the Consumer Electronics Show in Las Vegas, Nevada (US) every year to stay on top of the latest technology and trends. Joli is also an Apple enthusiast. She owns the iPad 1 and the iPad 2, and has two iPhones. She's written several iPad books. She has an iPod Nano for listening to audiobooks at the gym and has penned several other Mac books in addition to this one, including *Mac Basics in Simple Steps* for Pearson Education.

In addition to writing, Joli teaches computer classes (both Apple and Microsoft) at the local junior college and works as a network administrator and web designer for North Texas Graphics. Joli has written over a dozen books for Pearson's *In Simple Steps* and *Brilliant* series and is currently serving as series editor on other authors' titles. In her free time she enjoys yard work, exercising at the local gym and teaching her cats, Pico and Lucy, tricks.

Dedication

Mom, it's been almost three years. We all miss you deeply.

Contents

Introduction

Welcome to *Brilliant Mac Basics*, a visual quick reference book that gives you a basic grounding on the way the Mac works, introduces the Mac OS X, and in particular the latest Lion version, and demonstrates how to use and get the most out of the bundled applications that you will find on your Mac – a complete reference for the beginner user.

Find what you need to know – when you need it

You don't have to read this book in any particular order. We've designed the book so that you can jump in, get the information you need and jump out. To find the information that you need, just look up the task in the table of contents or Troubleshooting guide, and turn to the page listed. Read the task introduction, follow the step-by-step instructions along with the illustration, and you're done.

How this book works

Each task is presented with step-by-step instructions in one column and screen illustrations in the other. This arrangement lets you focus on a single task without having to turn the pages too often.

Step-by-step instructions

This book provides concise step-by-step instructions that show you how to accomplish a task. Each set of instructions includes illustrations that directly correspond to the easy-to-read steps. Eye-catching text features provide additional helpful information in bite-sized chunks to help you work more efficiently or to teach you more in-depth information. The 'For your information' features provide tips and techniques to help you work smarter, while the 'See also' cross-references lead you to other parts of the book containing related information about the task. Essential information is highlighted in 'Important' boxes that will ensure you don't miss any vital suggestions and advice.

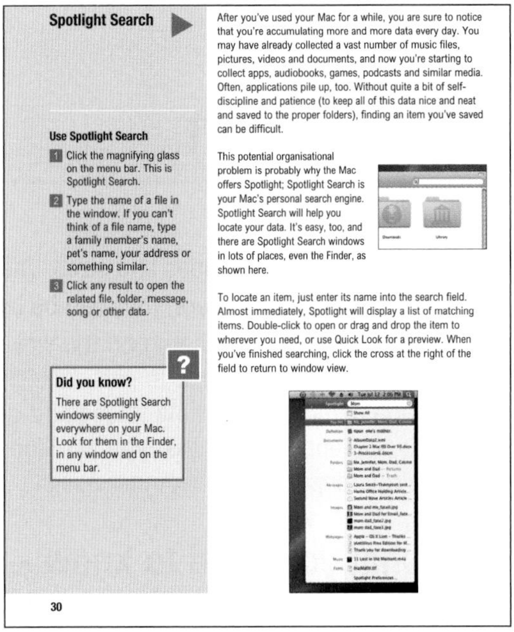

Troubleshooting guide

This book offers quick and easy ways to diagnose and solve common problems that you might encounter, using the Troubleshooting guide. The problems are grouped into categories that are presented alphabetically.

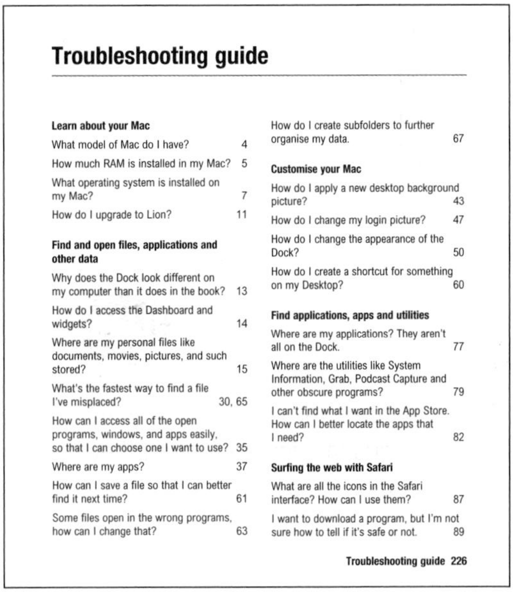

Spelling

We have used UK spelling conventions throughout this book. You may therefore notice some inconsistencies between the text and the software on your computer, which is likely to have been developed in the US. We have, however, adopted US spelling for the words 'disk' and 'program', as these are commonly accepted throughout the world.

Spotlight Search ▶

Use Spotlight Search

1 Click the magnifying glass on the menu bar. This is Spotlight Search.

2 Type the name of a file in the window. If you can't think of a file name, type a family member's name, pet's name, your address or something similar.

3 Click any result to open the related file, folder, message, song or other data.

Did you know? ❓

There are Spotlight Search windows seemingly everywhere on your Mac. Look for them in the Finder, in any window and on the menu bar.

After you've used your Mac for a while, you are sure to notice that you're accumulating more and more data every day. You may have already collected a vast number of music files, pictures, videos and documents, and now you're starting to collect apps, audiobooks, games, podcasts and similar media. Often, applications pile up, too. Without quite a bit of self-discipline and patience (to keep all of this data nice and neat and saved to the proper folders), finding an item you've saved can be difficult.

This potential organisational problem is probably why the Mac offers Spotlight; Spotlight Search is your Mac's personal search engine. Spotlight Search will help you locate your data. It's easy, too, and there are Spotlight Search windows in lots of places, even the Finder, as shown here.

To locate an item, just enter its name into the search field. Almost immediately, Spotlight will display a list of matching items. Double-click to open or drag and drop the item to wherever you need, or use Quick Look for a preview. When you've finished searching, click the cross at the right of the field to return to window view.

30

Troubleshooting guide

Know your Mac

1

Introduction

Apple Macs come in all shapes and sizes. They can be portable laptops or desktop computers; they can be large or small. Apple even offers a sleek all-in-one model that houses both the monitor and the computer in a single unit. The model you have probably depends on how you use it (and how much money you had to spend when you purchased it). If you use the Mac mainly at home or in a small office, you probably have a Mac mini or an iMac; if you travel a lot, you will have a MacBook instead. If you knew you'd need a lot of computing power, you may have purchased a Mac Pro.

All Macs though, whatever they look like on the outside, run some edition of the Mac OS X software on the inside. This software is what enables you to operate the computer; that's why it's called an *operating system!* That operating system (OS) software (called Mac OS X) can be upgraded and updated as time passes to keep it safe and secure and to add functionality as new features become available.

In this chapter, you'll learn about your own Mac and discover the model and OS X version, and you'll find out how to update it to keep it safe and secure for the long haul. You'll also learn how to upgrade the operating system so you can have all of the latest and greatest features when they become available. (If you think you know all about this already and are sure you're using Lion, feel free to skip to Chapter 2.)

See also

Confused about some terms here? Snow Leopard, Lion, Mac Mini or Mac Pro? Keep reading!

What you'll do

Discover your Mac model

Know what version of the Mac OS X software you have installed

Upgrade to Lion if you can

Get Mac updates for any OS version

Verify Software Updates is enabled

Mac models and specifications

▶

There are several Mac models and each comes with its own set of specifications (such as how much hard drive space is available or what type of unit the computer is housed in). It's important to know what model you have for several reasons. You may be asked to provide model information when getting help from a technical support technician from Apple or a repair shop, or you may want to answer a query from a friend or a relative who's interested in purchasing a Mac of their own. Additionally, when you know what kind of Mac you have, you can be sure that any hardware or software you purchase is compatible. This is especially important if you want to add memory to your Mac to make it perform better, or if you want to buy an adapter kit to mount your monitor to the wall. In that vein, here are the basic Mac models. See if you can figure out which model you have. If you're still not sure, work through the numbered steps to find out.

■ Mac Mini – this model is housed in a small, silver cube just a little more than 6in (16.5cm) square. You can easily hold it in your hands. When you get a Mac Mini, that's all you get. It does not include a monitor, keyboard or mouse. If you have one of these, make sure you place it somewhere it can 'breathe'. It needs a little room for air to stay cool and it's very tempting to hide it at the back of the desk or shelf where there's not enough circulation.

■ iMac – this model is a free-standing, all-in-one unit, containing a high-resolution LCD screen and a computer with plenty of processing power and hard drive space. This Mac comes with a keyboard and wireless mouse. This is an awesome machine, which takes up no space under the desk, as a computer with a tower would. There are also very few wires beyond the power cord and whatever you connect via USB.

- Mac Pro – this model is the typical desktop tower model with a separate display monitor. You generally set the tower under your desk and run cable from it to the monitor, keyboard and/or mouse. It's what most Windows PCs look like. The Mac Pro is a very powerful computer and is the best choice if you do a lot of video rendering and movie making, or otherwise need a powerful computer.

- MacBook – a MacBook is a laptop. You can choose from the MacBook, MacBook Air or MacBook Pro models. Of these three, the MacBook is the least expensive and offers the least amount of computing power, while the MacBook Pro is the most expensive and offers the most computing power.

Find your Mac model

There are several ways to find out what kind of Mac you have. You can go to the Apple website and look at the pictures of the Mac models, for one. You could go to an Apple store and do the same. You could dig out the paperwork you received when you purchased it, or look through the documentation. What's easier than all of that, though, is to click the Apple menu icon on the menu bar and click About This Mac.

Find your Mac model

1 Click the Apple icon on the menu bar.

2 Click About This Mac.

3 Click More Info in the resulting screen.

4 In the top line, under Hardware Overview, note the Model Name.

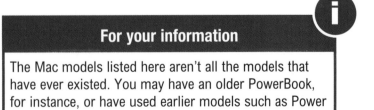

You'll also notice that you have access to much more information than just the model name. You can easily tell what kind of processor you have, the processor speed and the amount of memory, among other things. These are called 'technical specifications' and are detailed next.

For your information

The Mac models listed here aren't all the models that have ever existed. You may have an older PowerBook, for instance, or have used earlier models such as Power Macintosh or Performa.

Technical specifications detail how much memory your Mac has, how large the hard drive is, whether your Mac is capable of burning DVDs, and how many USB ports are available, among other things. But do you really need to know all the facts and figures and all the other gory details? Well, sometimes you do, because knowing this information can help you use your Mac more productively (finding out you have access to a built-in microphone or webcam, for instance), and identify where future problems might arise (such as running out of hard drive storage space).

Here are some things to look for in the technical specifications data:

- Under Hardware, click Audio (Built In). As you can see here, the Mac Mini offers a headphone jack, speaker, line input, external microphone and various display ports, among other things. Once you know what's available, you can make a point to use those features (such as connecting an HDMI-compatible monitor for better movie viewing).

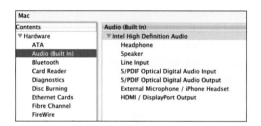

- Under Hardware, click Disc Burning. Find out whether your Mac can read and write to CDs and/or DVDs, and what compatible disks it can use.

- Under Hardware, click Memory. You'll have at least 2 GB of memory. That's enough for everyday computing tasks. However, if you find that your Mac is running sluggishly, you may be able to add more memory.

- Under Network, click AirPort. Here you can find out your Wi-Fi card type and current network information. This is good for troubleshooting network problems, should the need ever arise.

Did you know?

Try not to confuse memory with storage (that is, say, 4 GB of RAM with 160 GB of hard drive). What's the difference? Memory is where data is stored temporarily, the hard drive is where data is stored permanently (or until you manually delete it). A computer needs memory to store temporary instructions the computer must use, to send data to a printer, or to perform calculations. The computer needs a hard drive to save data you create and acquire, such as letters, pictures and music.

Know the technical specifications (cont.)

Memory	Status:	Connected
PCI Cards	Current Network Information:	
Parallel SCSI	**3802:**	
Power	PHY Mode:	802.11n
Printers	BSSID:	1c:af:f7:dd:b9:21
SAS	Channel:	5
Serial-ATA	Country Code:	US
Thunderbolt	Network Type:	Infrastructure
USB	Security:	WPA Personal
▼ Network	Signal / Noise:	−36 dBm / −91 dBm
	Transmit Rate:	130
AirPort	MCS Index:	15
Firewall	Other Local Wireless Networks:	
Locations	**Home:**	
Modems	PHY Mode:	802.11g
Volumes	BSSID:	0:1c:26:7a:63:52
WWAN	Channel:	1
	Network Type:	Infrastructure
	Security:	WPA2 Personal
	Signal / Noise:	−89 dBm / −73 dBm

Explore your Mac's technical specs

1 Click the Apple icon on the menu bar.

2 Click About This Mac.

3 Click More Info in the resulting screen.

4 In the top line, under Hardware Overview, select any option and review the information offered.

5 Repeat step 4 with Network and Software.

■ Under Software, click Applications. Find out which applications are installed on your Mac. You may find that you have applications you didn't even know about!

Jargon buster

You may see the following terms while browsing your Mac's technical specifications.

AirPort – Apple's 802.11b/802.11g standard for wireless networking.

Burning – the process of recording movies, music and data onto an optical disk such as a DVD or CD disks.

Cache – special memory that 'remembers' recent operations your Mac needs to function, thereby improving processing efficiency.

Hard drive – an area of your computer used to store data permanently.

RAM – random access memory used to hold data temporarily.

HDMI – High Definition Multimedia Interface that enables you to connect a superior display (monitor) for a better picture and viewing experience.

USB – universal serial bus ports that let you connect compatible devices, often mice, digital cameras, printers and scanners.

Firewall – a software mechanism for protecting the computer from Internet ills by assessing what's trying to come into your Mac. It does not let in data that is already known to be harmful.

Your Mac is a specific hardware model. It could be a laptop, desktop tower or all-in-one computing unit and it is probably (specifically) a Mac mini, a MacBook or an iMac. Whatever it is, it has an operating system installed on it. As noted previously, it's this operating system that lets you *operate* your computer's *system*. There are various versions of the OS X software, though, and what you have installed may be different from what I'm using in this book.

To understand how you came to have the OS X version you do, you need to know a little about the history of the OS X software. The Mac OS X operating system was introduced in 2001. Back then, from 2001 to about 2006 or so, Cheetah, Puma, Jaguar, Panther and Tiger were the code names of the available OS editions. Every OS X edition has had a code name. Those early versions were dubbed 10.0, 10.1, 10.2, 10.3 and 10.4 as well. These are version numbers. Since you probably don't have a Mac as old as this, I won't talk about them any more.

In 2007, OS X, version 10.5 was made available to the public. It was code-named Leopard. You may have a computer running Leopard if you purchased a Mac four or five years ago and never upgraded the operating system software. After Leopard, in 2009, Snow Leopard became available (10.6). Finally, in July 2011, Lion was introduced (10.7).

Mac OS X editions

1

Find your Mac edition

1 Click the Apple icon on the menu bar.

2 Click About This Mac.

3 Note the version number under Mac OS X.

4 Version 10.5.x is Leopard; version 10.6.x is Snow Leopard; version 10.7.x is Lion.

Did you know?

OS X is pronounced OS Ten.

Mac OS X editions (cont.)

It's very important that you understand that each new upgrade to a Mac OS X operating system version is an improvement in many ways. As an example, Lion offers 250 new features not available in Snow Leopard. Some of these improvements are beyond what you might expect. For instance, Lion lets you install a trackpad (or use the one on your MacBook) to incorporate new multi-touch gestures. You can use the App Store just as you're used to doing on your iPhone or iPad and install, access and use apps easily with the new Launchpad feature. You can access everything you have open at once on a screen called Mission Control, and you can enjoy features such as Auto Save and AirDrop (an easy way to share files with other nearby Mac users). The point is that if you can afford an OS upgrade, get it! The new features you'll have access to will be worth it.

For your information

OS X is a Unix-based operating system comprising two layers: the underlying Unix foundation that you don't ordinarily see and the highly intuitive graphic interface that you do. It's the graphical OS interface that lets you manipulate the computer with a mouse, menus, drop-down lists and dialogue boxes, among other things. If you hear the word Unix now, at least you'll know what it refers to.

Did you know?

Each step up the OS X version ladder is an upgrade. Each upgrade has more features and is more secure than the previous OS version.

For your information

After this chapter we'll be using Lion, the latest OS X version. However, if you have Leopard or Snow Leopard, this book will work for you too. I'll highlight Lion-specific features when they arise, so you'll know not to look for them.

As you know, I'm going to use Lion in this book and I think you should upgrade to Lion if possible. If I've convinced you with the list of tempting new features in the previous section, there are several ways to find out if your Mac is Lion-ready (and to get the upgrade). If you already have Snow Leopard (10.6) and have installed all of the latest updates (up to 10.6.8), your Mac is ready – you can simply work through the steps outlined here to get it. The upgrade costs about £30, and it's well worth it.

If you have an earlier version of the Mac OS X operating system software, you'll have to decide which upgrade options are available to you. For instance, if you have Leopard (10.5), you'll have to upgrade to Snow Leopard (about £30), and then upgrade to Lion once that's done.

Did you know?
You can access the App Store from the Apple icon on the menu bar.

Upgrade to Lion from Snow Leopard

1 Click the Apple icon on the menu bar.

2 Click About This Mac.

3 If you see version 10.6.8, continue here. If you see 10.6 but see something other than .8 (such as .4 or .6), update your software first as outlined in the next section, then return here.

4 Click the App Store icon on the Dock.

5 Locate Lion and click the price icon. Click Buy App.

6 Type your password (your Apple ID should appear automatically) and click Buy.

7 Wait while the process completes, which could take an hour or more.

See also
Learn how to check for updates in the next section, Update your Mac's OS.

Upgrade your Mac edition (cont.)

Mac OS X Lion

To set up the installation of Mac OS X 10.7, click Continue.

Continue

8 Once the download has completed, click Continue to complete the installation process.

9 Click Agree to agree to the software licence agreement. Click Agree again.

10 Click Install and type your password when prompted.

11 Allow your computer to restart once installation completes and wait for the rest of the installation process to finalise. You'll have to restart once more when this step is completed.

Important !

Not all Macs will be Lion-compatible and able to run Lion. Your Mac must have an Intel Core 2 Duo, Core i3, Core i5, Core i7 or Xeon processor to run Lion. As you know, you can find out whether your Mac has one of these processors by clicking the Apple icon at the top left of your screen, then choosing About This Mac.

Did you know? ?

When you upgrade your OS version, your data, settings, printers, network connections and other computer preferences remain intact and on your computer. You won't lose anything, so don't worry about upgrading!

For your information i

If you see 10.7, congratulations! You're running the most up-to-date OS available as of 2011.

No matter what version of OS X your Mac is running and has installed, you must check for and obtain updates for it. These updates keep your computer safe by protecting it from new-found security threats and security holes, by applying fixes for bugs and problems with existing components and installed software, and updates may even offer new features to older applications. Additionally, your Mac will need to be fully up to date to install operating system upgrades, such as Lion, introduced in the previous section (and whatever comes after Lion in a couple of years).

Manually check for updates for your Mac's OS

1 Click the Apple icon on the menu bar.

2 Click Software Update.

3 If updates are available, click Show Details. (This will change to Hide Details when you do.)

4 Most of the time you should install all of the updates. Make sure all are selected and click the Install button.

5 Agree to any software licences if applicable and reboot the computer if prompted to when the installation finishes.

For your information

You must be connected to the Internet to check for and obtain updates.

Update your Mac's OS (cont.)

Since you probably won't remember to check for updates regularly, Mac OS X has a built-in feature that checks for updates automatically. You should check to see whether your Mac is configured to do this. Here's how:

1. From the Dock, click System Preferences.

2. Click Software Update.

3. From the Scheduled Check tab, verify that your Mac will check for updates regularly.

Explore your Mac's graphical user interface

Introduction

Your Mac has lots of visual components you can use and manipulate. These components comprise the Mac's 'graphical user interface'. You use these components to do things such as open and use applications, play music, watch videos, send email and save files. The elements you'll use most include the Finder, which lets you navigate your Mac; open windows that hold your data and allow access to it; and the menu bar, which offers access to commands related to the active application or window. Quite often you'll also use the Dock (shown here), which runs across the bottom of the screen and offers easy access to your most used applications and data. If you've updated to Lion, you'll also use Mission Control and Launchpad quite often. There are even multiple desktops to configure and use. Of course, you can personalise all of these items to suit your needs.

What you'll do

Navigate your Mac with the Finder

Personalise the Finder

Understand what's available in a window

Use the menu bar

Get to know the Dashboard and configure widgets

Explore the Lion-only features Mission Control, Launchpad, Gestures and multiple desktops

Important

!

This is the Dock in Lion (OS X 10.7). If you have not upgraded to Lion you won't see all of the icons here. Also, if you've personalised the Dock, what you see will differ.

Another option for accessing features is the Dashboard. You can open it from the Dock – its icon is black and looks like an item you might see on the dashboard of a car. The Dashboard interface appears on the screen when you open it and the widgets it contains can include a clock, calculator, dictionary, calendar and similar items.

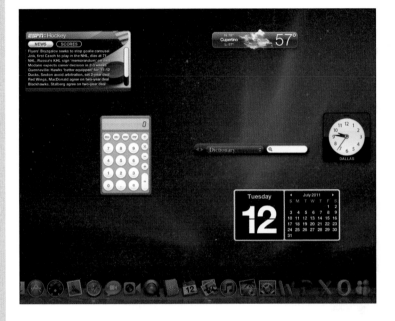

See also

Refer to Chapter 1 to learn how to upgrade to Lion.

For your information

Would you like to see the Dashboard in action? Click F12 on your keyboard. Click F12 again to make the Dashboard go away.

The Finder is where you'll go to navigate to files, folders, pictures or applications stored on your Mac, and where you'll search for data you've recently created, imported from a camera, or saved on a connected external drive (such as a USB flash drive or SD card). Basically, it's a place to locate your stuff. Beyond that, though, it's where you can perform system tasks such as ejecting a CD or DVD, accessing networked computers, or moving or copying files and folders from one area of your Mac to another. The Finder is really the heart of the Mac's graphical user interface.

The Finder icon is shown here. It's the one on the far left of the Dock and looks like a smiley face.

Finder

Open and explore the Finder

1. Locate the Finder icon on the Dock.

2. Click it.

3. If you have not upgraded to Lion, notice the items in the left pane, specifically:

   a. Macintosh HD

   b. Desktop

   c. Your user folder

   d. Applications

   e. Documents

2

Use the Finder (cont.)

4. If you have upgraded to Lion, notice the items in the left pane, specifically:

   a. All My Files

   b. AirDrop

   c. Desktop

   d. Your user folder

   e. Applications

   f. Documents

   g. Movies

   h. Shared

   i. iDisk

Did you know?

The Finder is always active in the background. To access the Finder window, click the Finder icon on the Dock. When other windows are open and you need access to the Finder on the menu bar, click an empty area of the desktop.

When you look at the Finder, you'll see components familiar to all windows you'll open on your Mac. There are Back and Forward buttons for navigation, options to change the view, options to take a quick look at a file, and access to contextual menus. There's also a Spotlight Search window where you can search for items.

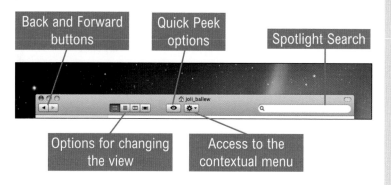

Back and Forward buttons

Quick Peek options

Spotlight Search

Options for changing the view

Access to the contextual menu

For your information

2

If you're moving from a Windows PC to a Mac, a contextual menu is what you're used to seeing with a right-click of the mouse.

If you've upgraded to Lion you'll see one additional icon. You can click this icon to change how the items in the window are organised. It's best to experiment with this now so you'll understand that what you'll see throughout this book and what you see on your computer can and will differ, depending on the views chosen. In the image here, for instance, I've sorted the items in my user folder (Home folder) by the date the data was last modified, but as you can see, there are many other options.

For your information

If you're using Lion, it might be best to configure your Home folder's view to show data by Name, for now.

Know what's available in the Finder (cont.)

In the left pane of the Finder you'll see various sections, too – what you see depends on how your Mac is configured and what OS you have. In the first image you can see Devices, Shared, Places and Search For. This is what's shown in Snow Leopard. Each of these has items under it. The second image is what you'll see in Lion. Notice here it's Favorites, Shared and Devices.

Here are some things you are likely to see in the Finder's Sidebar for pre-Lion Mac OS X editions, but what you'll ultimately see depends on how you've configured it:

- Macintosh HD (under Devices) – this offers access to everything on your Mac's hard drive. Although you could use this option for finding data on your Mac, clicking your user name under Places is much easier.

- Desktop (under Places) – this offers access to what's on your Mac's desktop.

- Your user's folder (under Places) – this is where you'll access your personal data.

- Applications (under Places) – you can access all installed applications here. Because you may later remove icons from the Dock for applications you don't use very often, it's important to know this is available.

- Documents (under Places) – this is where your documents should be saved and thus accessible.

- Today, Yesterday and others (under Search For) – click to quickly find data you've manipulated recently.

In Lion, look for these items in the Finder's Sidebar:

- All my files – you'll find all of your files here – it's a bit like the old Macintosh HD entry. Consider configuring this using Thumbnail view and sorting by Kind.

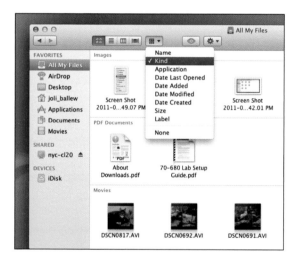

- AirDrop – a place to drag or place files so that others who also have an AirDrop feature on their Mac can access them when their computer is nearby.

- Desktop – click here to view the items on your desktop and work with them. Consider Thumbnail view and sort by Name to get started.

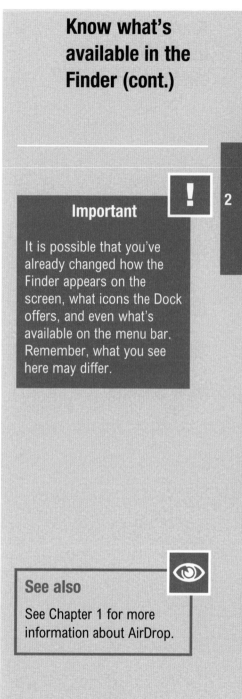

Know what's available in the Finder (cont.)

! 2

Important

It is possible that you've already changed how the Finder appears on the screen, what icons the Dock offers, and even what's available on the menu bar. Remember, what you see here may differ.

See also

See Chapter 1 for more information about AirDrop.

Know what's available in the Finder (cont.)

Explore the Finder

1 With the Finder open, click each item listed.

2 Insert an SD card or a USB flash drive. Note the change in the Finder.

3 Insert a CD or DVD. Note the change in the Finder.

4 Click Today; click Yesterday, if applicable.

5 To eject a USB stick, SD card or CD or DVD, click the triangular eject button that appears beside it.

■ Documents or Movies – click these folders to access what's in them.

■ iDisk – click to set up MobileMe, a service provided by Apple that lets you keep everying in sync on your Mac, PC, iPhone, iPad and iPod Touch. MobileMe is changing, so keep your eyes open for modifcations (specifically watch for iCloud).

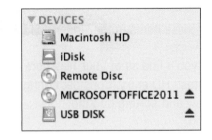

Did you know?

Folders are created and provided to you in a tree-like structure. You'll see Documents, Pictures, Movies and others. You can create your own folders and subfolders for managing your data, too. To explore this folder hierarchy, click your user name (Home folder), then click a subfolder in it (perhaps the Pictures folder), then click any folder in there (if applicable).

For your information

Under Devices in the Finder's Sidebar you can access any connected backup storage devices available to you. Icons will appear and will represent removable drives, iDisk (part of MobileMe) and any other data sources such as USB flash drives, SD cards or even MP3 players. To view the contents of any device, click its icon.

One way to personalise the Finder is to change the view. So far I've been encouraging you to use Thumbnail view, but there are others. You can change the view by clicking one of the view buttons at the top of the Finder window. Here's Cover Flow view. Once in this view, you can drag your mouse across the top pane to browse the available folders.

Change the view in the Finder

1 In the Finder, click any view options button.

2 Repeat to select another.

3 Continue until you've tried all four. In Lion, continue to experiment with the fifth view button to change how items in the window are sorted.

2

You can also customise the Sidebar by placing your most used items in the Places list in a pre-Lion version of OS X or under Favorites in Lion. You can select a folder you access often, for instance, and then drag it and drop it in the area you prefer. As you drag, the Finder highlights the Sidebar folders to indicate that dropping will place the item within that folder or else display a blue marker line to show that the shortcut will be created at that position. These two images show how it looks in Snow Leopard and how it looks in Lion.

?

Did you know?

You'll see something resembling a 'no entry' symbol when OS X won't allow you to drop a shortcut into a location that isn't suitable.

Personalise the Finder (cont.)

Add a folder in the Finder

1. In Finder, navigate to a folder you access often.

2. Drag the folder to the Sidebar.

3. Position the folder under the last item in the Places list or under the Favorites list, as applicable to your OS.

4. Look for the blue line to indicate where it will be placed.

5. Drop the folder there.

6. If desired, place an item in that new folder by dropping it on top of it.

Did you know?

To show the slider bar in Lion (as it's shown in the image here for pre-Lion OSes), click View and click Show Status Bar.

Finally, the Finder window has a number of buttons and other controls, some of which become highlighted as you scroll the mouse pointer over them. These buttons enable you to resize, reposition, close, minimise and maximise windows, toggle the Sidebar display and generally customise your view of the files and folders displayed within. Here are some helpful tips to help you learn to use these controls:

- Close, minimise, and maximise the Finder window by clicking the red, yellow and green buttons located in the top left corner of the Finder window.

- Toggle the Sidebar off and on by clicking the small, rectangular toggle button in the top right corner of the Finder window in pre-Lion OSes. In Lion, click View and then Hide Sidebar.

- Change the size of the thumbnails when in Thumbnail view by moving the slider left and right. The slider is located in the bottom right corner of the Finder window. In Lion, one way to change the size of thumbnails is to click Command + J and move the slider under Icon size.

- Click and drag from the bottom right corner of the window (or any corner in Lion) to resize the window manually.

Note that when the Finder is active (or when you've clicked an empty area of the desktop), the menu bar shows Finder options. One of the options under the Finder menu is to set the Preferences for the Finder. If you don't see the menu bar shown here, click the Finder's title bar to make it active or click an empty area of the desktop.

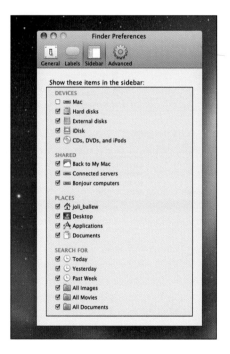

Configure Finder Preferences

1 Click the Finder's title bar to make it active if applicable or click an empty area of the desktop.

2 From the menu bar, click Finder and click Preferences.

3 Click the General tab.

4 Choose what to show on the desktop and what folder the Finder window should open with. (If you've just moved to Lion from Snow Leopard, you may want to select your Home folder here.)

5 Click the Sidebar tab.

6 Configure which items you'd like to see on the Sidebar.

7 Click Advanced and make any other changes as desired.

8 Click the red X in the top left corner of the Finder Preferences dialogue box to close it.

2

Work in open windows

You've already learned a little about windows because the Finder is housed in one. Every window has some of the same options, though, no matter what is open in it, including the ability to resize the window by dragging from the corner, minimising, maximising, and closing the window using the red, yellow and green buttons in the top left corner, and changing the view using the available view icons. There are a few more features, including accessing contextual menus, incorporating quick looks and more. Since you're already familiar with the Finder window, let's look now at the Applications window. Just open the Finder as usual, then click Applications in the Sidebar. Now proceed to explore the window as outlined in the panel here.

Explore more window controls

1. Open the Applications window.
2. Click the List icon to see List view. It's next to the Thumbnails button.
3. If you see a right-facing triangle in the results, click it to see additional items.
4. In the Sidebar of the Finder, click Documents.
5. If you have any documents, click one of them once.
6. Click the Quick Look icon – it looks like an eye.
7. Note the preview that opens.
8. Continue exploring as desired.

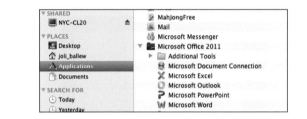

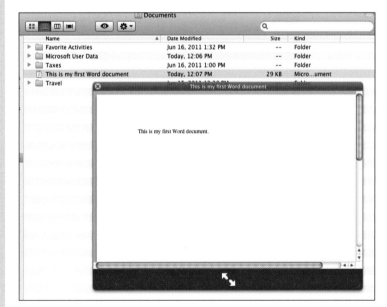

?

Did you know?

You can open a file's contextual menu with the keyboard combination Control + mouse click (or right-click + mouse click on a Windows keyboard).

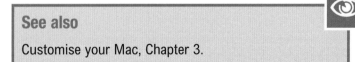

See also

Customise your Mac, Chapter 3.

While you're exploring the various windows and views, notice the Action button. It's to the right of the Quick Look button and is almost centred under the Finder's title bar. It looks like a wheel or a cog. When you click this icon you have access to what's called a *contextual* menu. The options you see in this menu may allow you to open a file, move it to the Trash, get information about the file, create a shortcut (alias), compress the file and more. If the file type is a picture, you'll also see the option to set it as your desktop picture (or background).

Explore contextual menus

1 Open the Finder.

2 Click your Home folder (that's your user name) and click Pictures.

3 Locate any picture on your Mac and select it. (Don't open it.)

4 Click the Action button in the Finder or use Control + click to view its contextual menu.

5 Click Get Info.

6 Review the information. Note that you can rename the file under Name & Extension, shown here, but make sure you keep the extension (.png, .jpg, etc.).

7 Select any other item, perhaps an application, document or music file. Explore its contextual menu.

?

Did you know?

If you have a two-button mouse you can access the contextual menu by right-clicking.

Explore your Mac's graphical user interface 25

Explore the menu bar

The menu bar is a small, transparent bar that runs across the top of your Mac's screen. It's the bar with the Apple icon on it, the volume icon and information about the network you're connected to, among other things. The menu bar also offers menus you can click to access the tools and features underneath.

Menus (and menu bars) are a fundamental element of any computer operating system or computer application and always provide you with standard and application-specific menu options. For instance, when you have a word-processing program open, your Mac's menu bar will almost always offer access to a File menu with various options such as Save, Save As, New, etc. You'll probably also have access to an Edit menu and maybe even a Format menu. These are common menu titles. Likewise, when the Mac's Finder is active, the Mac's menu bar provides menus, including File, Edit, View and others which enable you to open new Finder windows, view the Finder in various ways and perform similar tasks. After you use the menu bar for a while, you'll start to notice a pattern in menu titles and what's offered underneath them.

It's important to note that Lion has a new feature called Auto Save, so sometimes you won't see the familiar Save and Save As, for instance when you're viewing a picture in Preview. In these cases, look for other options, such as Save a Version, Duplicate or Export. Export is probably what you're looking for and offers you the familiar Save As option dialogue box.

The Apple menu

The icon at the far left side of the menu bar is the Apple menu. The Apple menu is always available, regardless of what else is running, giving you access to important system tools and information all the time, no matter what you're doing. You explored the Apple menu in Chapter 1, when you were figuring out what version of OS X your Mac was running and what kind of Mac you have purchased. It's also where you check manually for updates to the operating system. There's more to the Apple menu, though, including quick access to:

- the App Store, provided you have a compatible OS X version

- System Preferences, where you can configure a desktop background, screen saver, set up a home network, connect a Bluetooth device and create accounts, among other things

- Dock settings, including hiding or showing the Dock, changing its position on the screen and setting Dock Preferences

- options to turn on or off location services that help your Mac figure out where in the world you are

- recent items you've created or accessed

- options that allow you to make an application close (Force Quit) and the ability to cause your Mac to sleep, restart or shut down. You can also log off here.

Use the Apple menu to put your computer to sleep (among other things)

2

1. Click the Apple menu on the menu bar.

2. Review the options.

3. Choose Sleep if you don't need to use your computer for a while.

4. Choose Restart if you need to reboot your Mac.

5. Choose Shut Down if you won't need to use your Mac for a few days.

6. Choose Log Out if you want to secure your Mac while leaving it on and ready.

Did you know?

In all versions of OS X, the Mac's menu bar is a permanent fixture. While you can easily hide the Dock and the Finder's Sidebar, among other things, hiding the menu bar takes much more work (far more than you'd probably like to tackle).

Explore the
menu bar (cont.)

Use the menu bar to rearrange the icons in a window

1. Open the Finder and open any folder that contains data.
2. Click the View menu.
3. Click Arrange By.
4. Click Size.
5. Repeat and choose additional Arrange By options.

More menus

There are additional menus available for the Finder, specifically File, Edit, View, Go, Window and Help. If you'll take the time to look at the options under each of these menus now, you'll have a better feel for what to expect from menus with the same titles under different circumstances. Briefly:

- The File menu provides access to common actions associated with files and folders. You can create a folder, copy an item to the Sidebar or move it to the Trash (although nothing is actually deleted until you select Empty Trash from the Finder menu). You can also eject a removable device such as a CD or memory stick or burn an optical disk (CD or DVD, depending on your Mac's hardware).

- The Edit menu lets you cut, copy and paste data and undo edits you've already made. You can use it to 'Select All' of something or to show the Clipboard (which holds items you've cut and copied temporarily).

- The View menu lets you choose the way files and folders are displayed. You're familiar with some of the options such as List, Icons and Cover Flow. The Show Path Bar option lets you add a path display to the information bar in a Finder window (and you can switch it off with Hide Path Bar). You can also access a number of desktop customising options here, including the option to arrange the items in a view by name, date modified and other criteria.

- The Go menu is an aid to navigation offering direct routes to your Home folder, the Applications folder, other computers if your computer is attached to a network, iDisks (for those with .Mac accounts) and so on.

- The Window menu lets you minimise a window, zoom in on a window, cycle through windows, and even bring all windows to the front.

- The Help menu offers, well, help. Type what you're looking for in the Search box offered when you click Help and you'll be directed to an answer.

How (or whether) you use any or all of these menu bar options, combine them with navigational and editing shortcuts from other parts of the Finder or use them exclusively depends entirely on how you prefer to work. Most of the options feature keyboard shortcuts that are listed alongside the command. As you grow familiar with your Mac, you'll develop an operating style that's all your own.

Status icons

Look now to the far right side of the menu bar. You'll see various status icons. You'll probably see an icon for the volume button, to show the strength of a wireless network, the time, the date and a Spotlight Search icon (that looks like a magnifying glass). If you have Lion, you'll even see your user name, which lets you access other account names, view the Login window, and set user and group preferences. Click each icon and see what happens.

What you see when you click an icon depends on what you've clicked. If you click the Volume icon, you'll have the option to change the volume. If you click the Network icon, you can select a different network. If you click the time, you can change how the time appears on the menu bar (analogue or digital). If you click an icon from a third party, perhaps an icon placed there by an anti-virus software manufacturer, you can probably configure settings or open the program from there, too.

Spotlight Search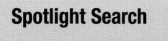

After you've used your Mac for a while, you are sure to notice that you're accumulating more and more data every day. You may have already collected a vast number of music files, pictures, videos and documents, and now you're starting to collect apps, audiobooks, games, podcasts and similar media. Often, applications pile up, too. Without quite a bit of self-discipline and patience (to keep all of this data nice and neat and saved to the proper folders), finding an item you've saved can be difficult.

Use Spotlight Search

1 Click the magnifying glass on the menu bar. This is Spotlight Search.

2 Type the name of a file in the window. If you can't think of a file name, type a family member's name, pet's name, your address or something similar.

3 Click any result to open the related file, folder, message, song or other data.

This potential organisational problem is probably why the Mac offers Spotlight; Spotlight Search is your Mac's personal search engine. Spotlight Search will help you locate your data. It's easy, too, and there are Spotlight Search windows in lots of places, even the Finder, as shown here.

To locate an item, just enter its name into the search field. Almost immediately, Spotlight will display a list of matching items. Double-click to open or drag and drop the item to wherever you need, or use Quick Look for a preview. When you've finished searching, click the cross at the right of the field to return to window view.

> **?**
>
> **Did you know?**
>
> There are Spotlight Search windows seemingly everywhere on your Mac. Look for them in the Finder, in any window and on the menu bar.

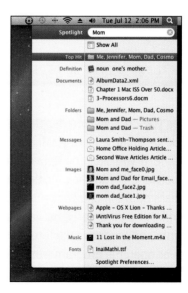

The Dock is one of the most appealing features of OS X and is extremely useful for those new to computing. It's also a speedy and intuitive starting point for anyone switching from another operating system (for instance from Microsoft Windows to a Mac). The Dock offers at-a-glance access to applications, folders, the Trash and more. You can customise the Dock, add your own stuff to it, remove what's there and place it somewhere else on the desktop if you like. If you have trouble seeing what's on the Dock, you can even magnify it.

Apple populates the Dock with what it believes is a representative selection of applications and utilities that you'll want to use. Not all of the applications on your Mac are there. However, there is Safari and Mail, iTunes, Address Book, iCal, FaceTime, iPhoto and more.

Important

Because you can easily remove items from the Dock (just drag them off onto the desktop), it's important to know that you can access anything formerly on the Dock from the Finder. Look in the Applications folder if you don't see an application you're supposed to see.

For your information

The names of items in the Dock are displayed as you move the mouse over them.

Use the Dock

Personalise the Dock

1. Locate the Dock that appears at the bottom of your screen and move the mouse over the icons.

2. To launch an application from the Dock, click its icon.

3. Control + click to access an icon's contextual menu options.

4. To reposition an icon on the Dock, drag and drop it to a new area on the Dock.

5. To remove an icon from the Dock, drag it off the Dock.

6. To add an icon to the Dock, locate it in the Finder and drag it to the Dock.

7. To move the Dock to another area of the screen:

   a. From the menu bar, click the Apple menu.

   b. Click Dock.

   c. Click a new position.

Use the Dock (cont.)

8 To magnify the icons on the Dock when you hover over them:

a. From the menu bar, click the Apple menu.

b. Click Dock.

c. Click Dock Preferences.

d. Enable magnification and use the slider to increase the size.

Did you know?

If an icon is bouncing up and down, it's opening. If an open application bounces, it needs your input.

For your information

If an icon has a shiny circle under it, it's already open.

The Dashboard is a hidden feature that offers 'widgets' you can use to quickly get information and perform common tasks. Default widgets include a calculator, a weather app, a calendar app and a clock. There are two ways to make the Dashboard appear: you can click the Dashboard icon on the Dock or you can press F12 on the keyboard.

Widgets differ depending on what they offer. Some widgets don't need a connection to the Internet to function properly; some do. For instance, your Mac can perform calculations on its own (and thus the Calculator app works fine without an Internet connection). However, some apps need the Internet to function. You'll need an Internet connection to get updated weather information, sports scores and information about flight delays, traffic, etc since there's no way your Mac could gain that information otherwise. Some widgets have preferences that you can customise, too. You can hover the mouse over a widget to find out if it's customisable. If an i appears in the lower right corner, click it; it's customisable. The widget will *flip over*, displaying its options.

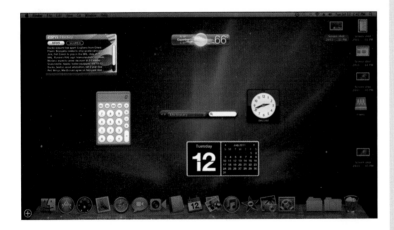

For your information

Some widgets, such as the calculator, are interactive and accept user input. Others offer a small i in the bottom right corner that enables you to personalise them.

Use the Dashboard and configure widgets

Use the Dashboard

1 Press the F12 key on the keyboard or click the Dashboard icon on the Dock. (This image is from Snow Leopard, but the Dashboard on Lion is very similar.)

2 Notice the widgets that appear on the desktop. Using the mouse, click a few numbers on the Calculator.

3 Explore the other widgets available. Later you'll add new widgets.

For your information

You have to customise widgets so they will be personalised to you. You must tell the weather widget which city you live in, for example.

See also

Visit Apple's widget pages at www.apple.com/downloads/dashboard for thousands more downloadable widgets.

Use the Dashboard and configure widgets (cont.)

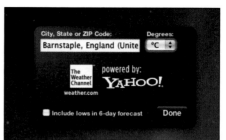

Configure or delete a widget

1 Open the Dashboard.

2 Hover the mouse over each icon. If you see a small i, click it to configure the item. (Many items won't have configuration options.)

3 Configure the widget as desired. Click Done if applicable.

4 To delete a widget, click the + sign near the Dock.

5 Click any X to remove the widget. Likewise, click any widget to add it.

6 Click the + sign in the bottom left corner. Click any widget to add it to the Dashboard.

7 Click the + sign again to close the add widget options.

8 Click the title bar of any widget and drag it to place it somewhere else on the screen.

9 Click an empty area of the desktop or press F12 to close the widget screen.

Did you know?

In the System Preferences app, under Expose & Spaces, you can change the keystroke required to invoke the Dashboard and choose any other Function key.

Lion's Mission Control offers a bird's-eye view of everything open on your Mac. It's Command Central and brings together the Dashboard, Spaces, Expose and full-screen apps so that you can see everything at once. If you aren't familiar with all of these terms, that's OK, you'll learn about them as you continue through this book and as you learn more about your Mac. What you want to do here is to invoke the Mission Control screen and explore it. To make Mission Control appear, click its icon on the Dock. For best results, open a few programs first so you can see all the features of Mission Control. Once in Mission Control, click any icon available to access it.

Mission Control has various parts:

- The top left item in the Mission Control screen offers access to your Dashboard widgets.

- The next item across the top of the screen is the desktop.

- If you see other items across the top of the screen, these are apps you can view in full screen.

- The Dock appears across the bottom of the screen.

- In the middle are your open applications, web pages, documents, pictures and other items.

?

Did you know?

If you have a trackpad you can swipe up with three fingers to open Mission Control. If you have a Magic Mouse, just double-tab the mouse surface. If you prefer to use a keyboard shortcut for opening Mission Control, you can use the default, which is a two-finger keyboard combination Control + ↑.

i

For your information

If you need more room for your windows and documents, you can create new desktop spaces. Create a space by dragging any app to the top row of the Mission Control interface. You'll see two desktops now and you can click either to access what's on it.

Use Lion's Mission Control (cont.)

Invoke Mission Control

1 Open some programs, apps and Safari.

2 If you have a trackpad, use three figures to swipe up. If not, click the Mission Control icon on the Dock or use the keyboard combination Control + ↑.

3 Click any item to access it.

4 Invoke Mission Control again using any method.

5 Drag any icon to the top of the Mission Control screen.

6 Note the new 'Desktop' entry.

7 Click that entry to view that screen.

8 Invoke Mission Control again.

9 Click the other 'Desktop' entry to see the other screen. You can move to this desktop through Mission Control or with gestures, detailed later.

10 To delete the extra desktop, hover your mouse over it and click the X that appears.

Did you know?

You can configure Mission Control preferences in System Preferences. You'll learn about System Preferences later in the book.

The App Store lets you purchase and download apps. Apps are small programs that let you do things such as keep track of the calories you've eaten in a day, play a game of Scrabble with a friend, compare prices for an item you'd like to buy, even order food online. You'll acquire apps and you need a place to access them. That's what Launchpad is for.

As with other Lion-only features, there are lots of ways to open Launchpad. You can open it from the icon on the Dock, of course, and you can configure a Hot Corner as well. I've set a keyboard shortcut to open Launchpad by tapping F3 on the keyboard (System Preferences>Keyboard>Keyboard Shortcuts>Show Launchpad). If you have a trackpad, you can position three fingers and your thumb on the trackpad, and make a gesture as though you're picking something up.

When you invoke Launchpad, if there's more than one screen of apps available, you can use your finger to swipe left and right on a trackpad, or use the arrows on the keyboard to move from page to page. You can also click the white dots that appear on the Launchpad. Once you've found the app you want, you simply click it. You close Launchpad using your key combination or by pressing Esc on the keyboard.

Explore apps with Lion's Launchpad

2

Explore apps with Lion's Launchpad (cont.)

As with other features on your Mac, Launchpad is customisable. You can:

- drag icons for apps to any other area of Launchpad
- drag icons for apps on top of another, similar app, to create an app group (folder)
- drag an icon for an app to the Dock
- delete an app you've acquired from the App Store by clicking, holding and then clicking the X that appears.

Did you know?

The Launchpad icon on the Dock looks like a rocket ship.

Jargon buster

Hot corner – something you configure that allows you to position your mouse in a specific corner of the scren to cause something to happen – perhaps for the Dashboard or desktop to appear.

A trackpad is a device you use instead of (or alongside) a mouse to navigate and use your Mac. If you have a laptop, you have a trackpad. I strongly encourage you to acquire a trackpad for your Mac if you don't have one, which you won't if you use a desktop computer. The new multi-touch gestures you can use in combination with Lion are fantastic and will make using your Mac easier. It'll also give your 'mouse hand' a little rest.

The names of the gestures available describe what the gesture actually requires you to do with your fingers. You can probably tell easily what a pinch, tap, touch or swipe would involve. You can use these gestures in practically any window and in various applications and apps, and you can practise those gestures now.

> **!**
> ## Important
> A tap on an external trackpad isn't like a tap on an iPhone or iPad. You actually have to tap hard. You'll feel the trackpad respond with a very light click.

> **?**
> ### Did you know?
> Expose is a feature that enables you, with a single keystroke or gesture, to view all open windows, windows of the current application only, or as small thumbnails. You configure your preferences in System Preferences. Expose (and its counterpart Spaces) isn't covered in this chapter, mainly because newer Lion features such as Mission Control, Launchpad and gestures are often better for locating what you want quickly and require far less user configuration. However, if you have a pre-Lion OS, open System Preferences and review the options under Expose & Spaces to learn more.

Use multi-touch gestures with a trackpad

Try multi-touch gestures on a trackpad

1. Use a single finger to move the cursor on the screen.
2. Tap on any item once to select it. Really tap it hard; don't just touch it.
3. Double-tap any item to open it.
4. Tap with two fingers to open a contextual menu (this is like a right-click or a Control + click).
5. Tap, hold and drag to move any item.
6. Touch (not tap) with two fingers and move them in a circular motion to rotate an item (such as a picture).
7. Touch (not tap) with two fingers and move them up or down to scroll through a web page or window that contains data that runs longer than a single page.
8. Touch with four fingers and drag from left to right to switch to another application.
9. Touch with four fingers and drag up and down to invoke Expose.

With gestures, explore multiple desktops

You have learned that while using Mission Control you can create multiple desktops and access them. If you're getting used to using gestures on a trackpad, you also know you can use three fingers to swipe up to get to the Mission Control screen (and down to exit). Once at Mission Control, position your mouse over the top right corner of Mission Control and click the + sign, shown below. Once you've added the desktops you want, you can click them in Mission Control to go there.

Now, the great part about having multiple desktops is that you can use your trackpad to swipe with three fingers left and right to access them. You can have applications open on each screen, too. This means that you can use the swiping method to move from app to app (really from desktop to desktop), while still having access to the items you actually store on your desktop. Desktop items appear on every desktop. You can use the same three-finger swipe to move between full-screen apps.

For your information

To delete a desktop, open Mission Control, position your mouse over the desktop to delete and click the X.

Customise your Mac

Introduction

Since its first incarnation, the Mac has offered options for customising; it's a machine you can truly make your own. You can change almost anything about it – you can alter the font size and colour, the desktop picture ('wallpaper'), set and configure a screen saver, change what's shown on the toolbar, personalise the Dock, and more.

While you might think that customising is something you do for fun or to pass the time while you're waiting for an important email or phone call, there's actually nothing frivolous about making a computer your own by adapting its appearance or changing how it behaves. A computer that's set to operate in the way you prefer will be far more enjoyable to use and is less likely to frustrate you (when features don't perform the way you'd like them to). A pretty desktop picture or a screen saver that hides your work from prying eyes is always a nice touch, too. All of this is especially useful if you work at your computer for hours at a time.

Finally, working through the personalisation options is a great way to get to know your Mac and that's why I've put it towards the front of the book. You'll learn a lot about dialogue boxes, making choices from a list of options, moving among open windows and more. By the time you've worked through this chapter you'll feel like a pro and your Mac will look and feel exactly the way you want it to.

What you'll do

Understand how to open and use the System Preferences pane

Change your desktop picture

Apply a screen saver and configure Hot Corners

Change your login picture

Add and remove items from the menu bar

Change the size of the Dock

Explore Dock stacks

Explore additional System Preferences

For your information

Some of you will already have experimented with some of the options you can change in Chapters 1 and 2, such as adding and removing items from the Dock and enabling Dock magnification.

Explore the System Preferences pane

Most of the changes you'll make to your Mac you'll configure in the System Preferences pane (which looks like a window or a large dialogue box). You access System Preferences by clicking the System Preferences icon on the Dock.

What you see in the System Preferences pane depends on which version of the Mac OS you're using. If you have Lion you'll have access to Lion-specific entries such as Mission Control and Launchpad. If you're not using Lion, you won't see these options. This figure shows Lion's System Preferences pane.

Navigate the System Preferences pane

1 Open System Preferences by clicking its icon on the Dock.

2 In the System Preferences pane, under Personal, click Dock.

3 Review the settings, and make changes if desired.

4. Click Show All to return to the main System Preferences pane.

When you click any icon in the System Preferences pane, the view changes and offers items unique to the clicked-on feature. For instance, If you click the Dock icon, the Dock configuration options will appear along with a new Show All button. You can configure Dock options here, and when you've finished you'll click Show All to return to the main System Preferences pane.

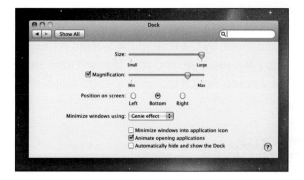

The desktop picture, which is often referred to as wallpaper or desktop background, is what appears on the screen when there are no open windows or, if windows are open, the picture that appears behind them. You change the desktop wallpaper in System Preferences. You can choose from various pictures Apple provides, you can choose photos from a folder you've created in iPhoto (see Chapter 9), or you can choose photos from any other folder on your hard drive.

If you'd like to make your desktop a sort of running slide show of your favourite pictures, first copy those pictures to a folder you create and name that folder something like My Favourites. (See Chapter 4 to learn how to do this.) Then click the + sign in the Desktop & Screen Saver pane, locate the folder and add it to the list, then select it. Now you can tell your Mac you want it to show those pictures as your desktop wallpaper and you'd like the picture to change every so often. Here, I've selected the pictures in a folder I created called My Favorites and I've opted to change the picture every 5 seconds.

Change your desktop picture

Set the desktop wallpaper

1. Click the System Preferences icon in the Dock.
2. Select Desktop & Screen Saver from the Personal category.
3. Verify that the Desktop tab is selected.
4. Under Apple, click Desktop Pictures, Nature, Plants, Art and any other folders there.
5. If you see a picture you'd like to apply, click it.

3

Did you know?

When you choose multiple photos to serve as your desktop wallpaper, you also configure how long to leave one picture up before changing to the next.

Apply a screen saver and configure Hot Corners

Select and apply a screen saver and configure Hot Corners

1. From System Preferences, select Desktop & Screen Saver.
2. Click the Screen Saver tab.
3. Click on any screen saver in the list to view it.
4. If desired, click Test.
5. To configure options for the screen saver you like, click Options.
6. Configure options as desired and click OK.

! Important

Third-party desktop screen savers, like the aquarium screen saver mentioned here, that can't be accessed from the Desktop & Screen Saver pane in System Preferences may be unable to be configured with a password or applied to Hot Corners and can't incorporate your Mac's other default screen-saver options.

It used to be that screen savers protected your computer from 'burn-in', where a picture would get burned into the screen if left on the monitor for too long. (The same sort of thing happens if you stare at something for a very long time and then close your eyes – you can still see the image!) Screen burn-in doesn't happen any more, but that hasn't lessened the importance of screen savers or their popularity.

One of the ways you can use a screen saver effectively is to protect your computer when you've left it alone for a specific period of time that you set. You can configure a screen saver to be applied after, say, 30 minutes of inactivity, and then in the Security settings require that a password be entered to view the screen again. If you're not worried about nosy co-workers or family members, though, screen savers can still be a nice touch. For instance, my Mac offers a Word of the Day screen saver, iTunes Artwork screen saver and even a screen saver that enables me to type a message that appears on the screen (perhaps 'You're Brilliant!').

Finally, you can buy *desktop* screen savers that offer realistic, moving fish in an aquarium, among other things, although they may not be 'true' screen savers and you may not be able to access them from the Desktop & Screen Saver pane. Here's a desktop screen saver I enjoy called Desktop Aquarium 3D; you can't actually see the fish moving in the screen shot here, but these fish are indeed swimming around on my desktop.

Once you've selected and applied a screen saver from the System Preferences pane, one way to cause the screen saver to be applied is to simply let the computer sit idle for the required amount of time. For instance, if you configure the screen saver to be applied after 30 minutes of inactivity, simply wait 30 minutes.

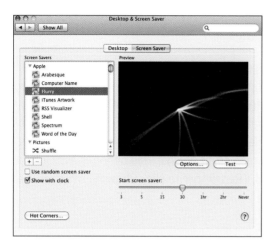

Apply a screen saver and configure Hot Corners (cont.)

7 If desired, select Show with clock.

8 Move the slider to configure how long to wait to apply the screen saver.

9 Click Hot Corners.

10 Configure Hot Corners as desired and click OK. (By default, the left screen corner is configured to invoke the screen saver.)

11 Click Show All.

3

! Important

To use a Hot Corner, you must move your mouse cursor to that corner of the screen. In the case of the screen saver, position your mouse just to the left of the Apple icon on the menu bar as far into the corner as possible, moving it almost off the corner of the screen.

? Did you know?

Just as you can select multiple pictures to use as desktop wallpaper, so can you choose multiple pictures to serve as a screen saver. If you wish, review the picture folders available in the Screen Saver options and select a folder. You can also add a folder as outlined in the previous section and even shuffle any pictures you choose.

Apply a screen saver and configure Hot Corners (cont.)

If you'd like to make the screen saver to come on at the exact moment you've finished working or because you need to leave the room for a moment, you can configure a Hot Corner. Hot Corners provide a shortcut for calling up the screen saver (or performing some other operation). When a Hot Corner is configured for the screen saver, you simply direct the mouse pointer to the proper Hot Corner and pause for a moment to cause it to engage.

Finally, if you are selecting and applying a screen saver for the purpose of protecting your computer, you'll want to require a password to be applied to disable it when you're ready to use your computer again. To do this, in System Preferences, click Security. Place a tick in Require password immediately after sleep or screen saver begins. This option is available under the General tab. (Remember to click Show All when you've finished.)

?

Did you know?

You can purchase and download screen savers from the App Store. You can access the App Store from the Dock and the Applications window.

You may know that your Mac automatically assigns a login image for all users. The choice is random, meaning your picture might be a paint palette even if you can't draw a straight line! It's easy to change the picture, though, especially if you opt for a picture provided to you by Apple.

1. Open System Preferences.

2. Click Accounts in pre-Lion OSes and Users & Groups in Lion.

3. Click the picture associated with your user name. Here, that's a paint palette.

4. Select a new picture.

You can also browse to a picture that you have on your hard drive and assign it as your login image. Before you try, though, make sure you know where your picture is stored, which is hopefully in the Pictures folder or a subfolder in it.

◄ **Change your login picture**

Use your own picture as a login image

1 Open System Preferences, and click Accounts (or Users & Groups in Lion).

2 Click the current picture and click Edit Picture.

3 Click Choose.

4 Locate the picture and click Open.

5 Use the slider to make the image fit in the window offered.

6 Click Set.

7 Click Show All.

3

ⓘ **For your information**

While browsing for the picture to use for a login image, opt for Thumbnail view – it'll make it easier to find.

Personalise the menu bar ▶

The menu bar is the bar that runs across the top of the screen. Beyond the menus you'll access to perform tasks are the 'informative' icons that tell you the time and date and offer various other kinds of information. On occasion, when you install a third-party program, it may attach itself here. Additionally, you may see new icons as you connect hardware, such as Bluetooth devices or hardware you use for backing up data on your Mac. Although it's highly unlikely the menu bar will ever appear cluttered, there still may be too many things on it (or not enough) for your liking. You can configure some of what's there already and tell certain items never to appear there at all.

First things first: take a look at what's on the menu bar now. Click the date and time and notice the options available to you. Here, you might opt to show the time as a digital or analogue display, or you may want to access the Date & Time Preferences pane (available in System Preferences).

Remove the Network icon from the menu bar

1 Click the Network icon on the menu bar.

2 Click Open Network Preferences.

3 Deselect Show AirPort status in menu bar (or Show Wi-Fi status in menu bar for Lion).

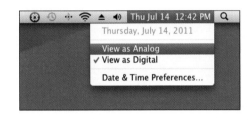

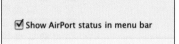

?

Did you know?

In the Date & Time Preferences pane, you can opt not to show the date and time on the menu bar.

!

Important

If the lock icon in any System Preferences window is locked, click it and enter your password to make changes.

Now, click the network icon on the menu bar, if it's available. The icon is shown here along with the options I see. What you see will differ. If you opt to access the Network Preferences pane, you can choose not to show this icon in the menu bar if you don't need to see it.

Finally, if you see an icon for a third-party program, perhaps an anti-virus program or something else that runs all the time, click it. If you see an option for Preferences, click that too. Depending on the program, you may or may not see an option to remove the icon from the menu bar.

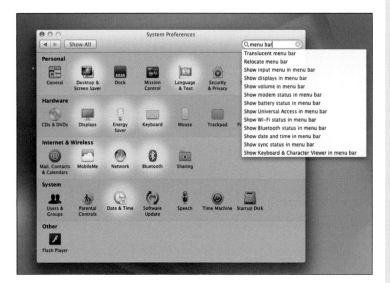

Explore menu bar options in System Preferences

1 Open System Preferences.

2 In the Spotlight Search window, type menu bar.

3 Note all of the options available (this image shows Lion). Click any option to access it.

4 Make changes as desired.

3

Change the size of the Dock ▶

You learned a lot about the Dock in Chapters 1 and 2, but you may not have explored every option. One of my favourites is the option to increase and decrease the size of the Dock. Another is to auto-hide the Dock so that it appears only when it's needed.

Since you're already familiar with accessing Dock Preferences from the Apple menu on the menu bar, and since you know that the Dock is available in the System Preferences pane, let's open Dock Preferences in a new way.

1. On the menu bar, type Dock in the Spotlight Search window.

2. From the results, next to System Preferences, click Dock.

3. Move the slider for Size to the left and to the right and watch what happens to the size of the Dock.

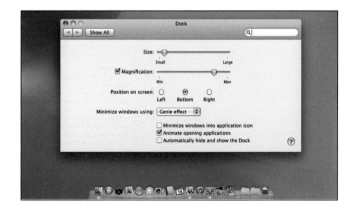

4. Next to Position on screen, click Left, then Right, then Bottom.

5. Select Automatically hide and show the Dock. The Dock will disappear. Move your mouse to the bottom of the screen to make it reappear.

6. Click Show All.

Stacks are groups of commonly used items you can access from a folder on the Dock. Your Mac comes with three built-in stacks: one for applications, one for documents and one for downloads. You can click any stack to see what's in there and click any item to open it. These folders and their resulting stacks of icons are available on the right side of the Dock, next to the Trash. Click any folder to see its contents.

If what you see doesn't look like what's shown here, Control + click the folder (or related icon). In the resulting list, select Sort by>Name, Display As>Folder and View content as>Automatic. When you do this, note the other options. You can opt not to view the content as it's shown here but instead view it as a fan, grid or list. Here's the same stack of applications displayed as a 'fan'.

Did you know?

It's easy to create your own stack. First, follow the directions in the next chapter to create a folder and populate it with data, such as documents, presentations or media. Next, drag the folder from the Finder to the right side of the Dock. Simple!

◀ **Explore Dock stacks**

Explore stacks

1 Locate the folders on the right end of the Dock.

2 Click any folder.

3 Take a look at what's available and click any item to open it.

4 To change how the stacks appear, Control + click (or right-click) the folder.

5 Choose new options as desired.

3

Important !

If you don't see the Applications, Documents and/or Downloads folder on the Dock you'll want to add them. For pre-Lion OSes, open Finder, click Macintosh HD in the left pane and type the name of the missing folder in the right. Drag that folder to the right end of the Dock and drop it there. For Lion, go to your Home folder and browse until you find what you want to add. Then drag it there.

Explore additional System Preferences

▶

There are many additional settings you can configure on your Mac. However, there's no need now to show you each and every one; you have the knowledge you need to continue personalising on your own. To find out just how much is available to configure, and to see how much you already know about configuring, open System Preferences and click these icons:

■ Appearance (pre-Lion) – note the options to change how many recent items appear in any recent items lists. If you're using Lion, explore General instead.

■ Expose & Spaces (pre-Lion) – see that you can configure active screen corners (Hot Corners), detailed earlier, and the shortcuts available to open all windows, application windows and the desktop.

■ Language (or Language & Text) – click the Formats tab to change how dates, times and numbers are displayed.

■ CDs & DVDs – click to change what happens when you insert a CD or DVD. For instance, when you insert a video DVD, the DVD player opens. If you'd rather that something else opened instead, you can choose it here.

■ Displays – click to change the display resolution.

■ Energy Saver – click to change when the computer and the display go to sleep.

■ Mouse – click to change the tracking and scrolling speeds or to set up a Bluetooth mouse.

- Trackpad – click to change trackpad properties or to install a Bluetooth trackpad. You can also view tips for using a trackpad, as shown here.

- Accounts (or Users & Groups) – click to change what happens when you log in to your Mac. You can opt to make specific programs open, for instance. You'll have to click the lock and enter an administrator's name and password to make changes to someone else's account, though.

Explore additional System Preferences (cont.)

Important

3

When you want to make changes to the system that your Mac deems a security threat, potentially harmful or an invasion of someone else's privacy, you'll have to click the lock icon and enter an administrator's user name and password first. This is especially true when you're in the Accounts section of System Preferences, or when you're configuring networking or sharing. If at any time you try to make a change but can't because the feature is greyed out or inaccessible, click this lock first.

Files, folders and managing your data

Introduction

When you use your computer, you're basically creating, amassing and/or processing information. Information, in computer terms, is referred to as data. The data you acquire, including pictures, Word documents, emails, music, videos, presentations, etc. must be organised so that you can find it when you need it and so that your Mac can find it when you ask for it. You (and your Mac) organise that data in folders.

Macs come with specific folders built in and there's a distinct folder hierarchy. You learned a little about this hierarchy in previous chapters; here you'll learn even more. You'll learn how to create shortcuts (aliases) for the folders you use most so that you can access them quickly, and how to move, copy and delete folders or the data you keep in them. You'll also learn techniques for managing your data by saving it, backing it up and securing it. Because data is really the heart of computing, you'll want to learn all you can about how to manage your data right from the start. And you'll want to know how to organise the data you keep so you can find it and back it up easily.

Did you know?

The earliest computers available to the general public had somewhere around 1 GB of hard drive space (or less) for storing files. Today's computers almost always come with 160 GB or more. This means you have plenty of space to hold your data, but it doesn't mean you don't have to manage it!

What you'll do

Understand how folders are organised

Create an alias for a folder

Save a file

Change which program a file opens with

Find data with Spotlight Search

Move, copy and delete files and folders

Compress data

Explore ways to auto-save your open files

Back up your data with Time Machine

Learn file and folder basics

Your Mac's folder system is organised in a very specific way. You may have some idea of this if you've ever clicked Macintosh HD in the left pane of the Finder on a pre-Lion OS X Mac. Lion doesn't offer the Macintosh HD icon any more, but for the purpose of this discussion it would be helpful if Lion users had access to it. That said, if you have Lion, do this before continuing:

1. Open Finder.

2. Click Finder>Preferences.

3. Click the Sidebar tab.

4. Place a tick by Mac under Devices.

5. Close the Finder Preferences window.

6. Under Devices in the Finder, click Mac.

7. Double-click Macintosh HD.

Now that you're able to access the Macintosh HD, you'll find five folders: Applications, Library, System, User Guides And Information and Users. These folders define the Mac's folder hierarchy and are the top-most organisational units. Inside these folders are related data. To understand this better, think of the Macintosh HD as a large filing cabinet and then picture these folders as its five drawers. Each drawer has folders (and maybe subfolders) and those folders store data. That's how your Mac is set up.

The folders store the following data:

- Applications – this is where programs installed on your Mac are stored. Although you can access applications here, it's probably easier to access them from the Applications folder on the Dock or the Applications folder in the Finder's Sidebar.

- Library – there are several Library folders. For the most part, the Library is managed and maintained by OS X and contains system-wide applications support files, fonts available to all users, data caches and other essentials that wise users (especially novices!) steer well clear of. There's also a Library folder in pre-Lion Home folders, which can contain fonts and certain other data accessible only to you.

- System – this folder contains the files belonging to OS X itself. It's best to leave this alone. Don't put anything into the System folder and don't take anything out of it.

- User Guides And Information – My Snow Leopard Mac mini came with this folder and it contains PDF files that offer information about your Mac, such as the User's Guide. Look inside your User Guides And Information folder to find out what's there.

Learn file and folder basics (cont.)

Explore the Macintosh HD and your personal Home folder

1 Open the Finder.

2 Click Macintosh HD. (Lion users, click Mac first.)

3 Open each folder, see what's inside and click the Back button.

4 Click your Home folder under Places or Favorites.

5 Click each folder to see what's inside and click the Back button.

6 Repeat until the folder hierarchy becomes clear.

Users – this folder contains the personal workspaces of all the users with accounts on the Mac. If you're the only user there'll be just two or three folders inside: yours, denoted in lower case by the short name you entered when you created your account, Shared, a kind of open-access workspace for any user (useful for swapping files between otherwise secure accounts) and Guest (if the Guest account is switched on). If you've created additional user accounts on your Mac so others can access it, you'll see their user folders as well.

Jennifer   joli_ballew   pico   Shared

Did you know?

If you open the Finder, browse to Users and then try to access another user's personal folders (such as Desktop, Documents, Movies, etc.), you'll probably get a message that states that the folder can't be opened because you don't have permission to see its contents.

For your information

Folders are used to contain and organise your files. Files are the documents, pictures, music, movies and any other data you save to those folders.

Now that you've explored the Macintosh HD folders, which you'll rarely access, let's take a look at your Home folder, which you'll access regularly. Your Home folder is your personal space on the Mac; it's where you put your files and folders.

Your Home folder contains a number of subfolders created by OS X, each marked with an icon relating to its function. For instance, the Movies folder has a film strip, the Pictures folder a camera, the Music folder a musical note and so on. Folders such as Desktop, Documents, Movies, Music and Pictures are there for you to use with appropriate data as you wish. You can upload pictures from your camera, for example, and you can store them conveniently in the Pictures folder; you can save a letter you've written to a friend in the Documents folder. While it isn't absolutely necessary to organise your data in this way, it certainly aids ease of use and security. With your files saved properly, you can keep them private and make sure they're quick to find and back up.

There are a few other folders in your Home folder, including Desktop, Downloads, Public and Sites. Pre-Lion OSes have Library too. You can explore these to see what's in them. Briefly, the Desktop folder contains the items you see on the desktop; Downloads is a place to store data from the Internet and other sources; the Library, rather like the Library at the Mac's root level, contains system-level data such as fonts and support files for applications, but which apply only to you; the Sites folder contains files associated with sharing data over a network using the same special protocols as the Internet; and the Public folder is a place for files that you want to share with other users who log into your machine or connect to it across a network. These users can see the contents of your Public folder and can copy items from it.

Explore your Home folder

4

Create an alias for a folder

An alias is a shortcut to a file, folder or application that's on your Mac. Aliases use very little disk space and you can create any number of them for a single item. This means that you can put aliases for your most used items anywhere you like, including on the desktop or in folders or subfolders.

If you can't immediately grasp how aliases could help you use your Mac more efficiently, consider this scenario. You use iMovie to make movies of video you shoot with your digital video camera and you like to store your movie-related files inside the iMovie Projects folder. This folder is a subfolder of the Movies folder. However, you have to leave the Movies folder to access other folders that contain data you need, such as videos, clip art, music, even other video-editing programs. If you create aliases for these in the Movie folder, you'll never have to leave it!

Create an alias and place it in the desired folder

1. Open the Finder and locate the folder or application for which to create an alias.

2. Control + click to access the contextual menu.

3. Click Make Alias.

4. Drag the new alias and drop it in the desired location.

Did you know?

Control + click on a Mac or Windows keyboard opens a contextual menu. You can also select the item and click the Settings icon in the Finder window, right-click a two-button mouse, or two-finger click on a trackpad to get there.

Important

There's a difference between moving a folder and creating an alias for one. An alias is simply a shortcut. You really shouldn't move default folders (or applications).

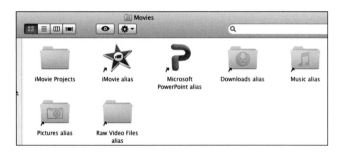

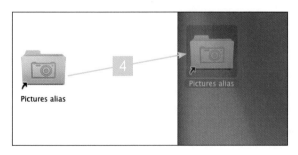

Although you may already know how to save a file to a particular folder, it would be remiss of me if I didn't include it here, along with some tips for keeping your Mac's data organised. This is an important topic because some people save everything to the desktop, which makes finding data more difficult, and I think they do that because they're unsure of how to save elsewhere (or whether they'll be able to find it later). While you can use Spotlight Search to locate something quickly and open it (no matter where you've saved it), that feature is not always available or useful, especially if you're using a third-party program and want to insert a picture or add a video clip into a file you're working on there, for instance. Ultimately it's best to take the time it requires to save files properly the first time you save them and to save them in an appropriate folder.

Almost every program will have a File>Save As option. Likewise, they'll probably all have File>Save. (In Lion, you may see File>Export.) You'll use these to save a file. The commands are different though. The first time you save a file you should select File>Save As because this gives you access to all of the 'save' options, including what type of file to save, where to save it and what to name it. Once you've saved the file, you can simply click File>Save to quickly save any changes you've made since. If you don't see a File>Save option, you're using Lion and Lion has already saved the data for you. If you'd like to save it somewhere specific, or configure precise save options, click File>Export. You'll see File>Export as the only option in Preview, if you'd like to explore.

Save a file to a folder

Save a file to a folder in TextEdit

1. Open the Finder, click Applications in the Sidebar and open TextEdit.

2. Type a few words.

3. On the menu bar, click File and click Save As. Click Save if that's all you see.

Important

When naming files, choose a name that will allow you to easily remember what it is, even if you look at it a year from now.

4

Did you know?

If you don't see where you want to save a file from the drop-down list, click the down arrow by the Save As window. This will expand the dialogue box and enable you to choose from additional options.

Save a file to a folder (cont.)

4 Name the file.

5 Click the arrow next to Where to see some of the places you can save the file. Click Documents, the default.

6 Click the arrow next to File Format to see the format options. Click Rich Text Format, the default. Note the other options, though; these are *file formats*.

7 Click Save.

See also

Lion has changed how files are saved and what options you have after a save has been applied. Lion's save options are detailed on pages 72–73.

Here, we have detailed how to save a file using a simple interface with only the most basic save options. You can see more options if you click the arrow next to Save As in this basic window. When you do this, you have access to additional navigational options, shown below. You can even access folders on shared drives on your home network, as I'm doing. This is a screen shot of a pre-Lion environment.

For your information

Once you've saved a document to a specific place using the Save or Save As command, all you have to do is use the key combination Command + S to save any future changes to the file. You can also access the Save command from the File menu. If you're using Lion, your file will be saved automatically every 5 minutes, and you'll have the ability to access any version of that file you like. Read on to learn more about Lion, detailed later in this chapter.

To open a file, say a word-processing file that you'd like to edit, you double-click it. If the associated program is not already running, OS X will launch it and then the file will be made available for you. (You can also select the file with a single click and press Command + O to get the same result.) The program that opens is the program that's currently associated with the file. However, this may not be the program you actually want to use. For instance, you may want all of your word documents in Microsoft Word, but they open in Apple's Pages instead. You may want to always open one specific document in Word and leave the others to open in Pages. Whatever the case, when this happens you need to change the file association for the item or file type. You set file associations in the Get Info options for a file.

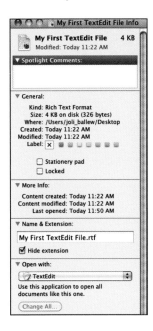

Jargon buster

Every file has an associated file type. Pictures are often jpegs and thus end in .jpg or .jpeg. Word files can be of various types but are often in Rich Text Format (.rtf), Word document (.doc) or even Portable Document Format (.pdf). You can see what type of file you have from the Get Info window.

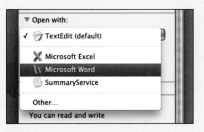

Open files and set file associations

Change which program a file opens with

1. Locate a file that opens in the wrong program.

2. Control + click (or right-click) to view the contextual menu.

3. Click Get Info.

4. If necessary, click the arrow by Open with to see the options.

5. Click the down arrow by the program that's currently being used to open the file and click the desired program.

6. If you want all of the files of the same file type to use this program, check Change All. (Change All will be greyed out if it's already the default program for other files of this type.)

7. Click the red X in the top left corner of the Get Info window.

Open files and set file associations (cont.)

?

Did you know?

You can drag and drop a file onto the icon of the application that you used to create it to open it. To open multiple items, select by Shift-clicking them and then drag and drop on the application icon. After selecting, you can also press Command + O to open them.

!

Important

If there's no associated application for a file (for instance when you've downloaded an item from the Internet), you'll be prompted to search through a list of likely candidates and select the one most suitable for you.

You should now be saving to the proper folders and experimenting with file formats and you can easily find your files when you need them. If you're not quite that organised yet (or are still a bit shaky when looking for folders and applications), you can find any file, folder or program using Spotlight Search. There are lots of Spotlight Search windows available on your Mac, including in the Finder, on the menu bar and even in the System Preferences window.

Since you've already explored Spotlight Search in the previous chapters, I'll introduce here just a few things you may not yet know about Spotlight Search.

◀ **Find data with Spotlight Search**

- Spotlight is a super-fast search tool that is always available. It maintains an index of every item on your Mac and uses metadata (data that describes it), such as creation date, file name and type, size and contents, to make searches almost instant.

- You can use Spotlight to search for all kinds of stuff as well as files. For instance, you can search for dictionary definitions or transcripts from iChat sessions, and you can even search for answers to simple mathematical problems by typing in an equation and getting Spotlight to solve it for you!

- Spotlight searches are dynamic; the Mac displays results as you type. The more you type, the more specific the results are.

- You can click any item from the list of results to open it. Alternatively, you can click Show All to open the results in a search window. You can also drag an item from the results window to the desktop (or to any other destination).

4

Find data with Spotlight Search (cont.)

■ You can tell Spotlight to search for something very specific by putting quotes around it. Then Spotlight will look for that exact phrase. For instance, 'Letter to Yvette' would offer a search that includes the phrase 'Letter to Yvette'. Without the quotes Spotlight would return all items that matched any part of the search string: 'letter', 'to' and 'yvette'.

■ You can incorporate Boolean operators such as AND, OR and NOT to perform advanced searches. If you're familiar with these operators, give them a try!

For your information

In any Spotlight Search list of results, click Show All to open a Finder window with all of the results displayed.

It won't be long before you outgrow the default folders that came with your Mac. That's OK – you can create your own folders and subfolders, naming them to meet your needs and manipulating them at will to suit the way you like to work. Of course, you'll also use those new folders to organise the files you want to save. You can create folders on the desktop, within your Home folder or nested within any other folders in your Home folder, for starters. You may decide, for example, to create a folder called Travel Plans and place it in your Documents folder, and create folders inside that for all the places you're planning to visit. Once you've built a folder structure you can start moving and copying the files.

Create and rename folders

Consider what type of data you save most, what kinds of data are the most important to you, and what data stands apart from everything else. Now, think of some folder names that would be appropriate to manage that data. For example, you may want to create subfolders for the Documents folder named Taxes, Classes, Projects, Legal, etc. and then create subfolders inside those (such as Taxes 2011, Taxes 2012 and so on, or English, Physics, Chemistry). With that done you can move on to your Pictures folder. You could create subfolders in the Pictures folder named Children, Pets, Hobbies, Weddings, Graduations, Holidays, etc., with related subfolders as applicable.

Manipulate files and folders

Create and name a folder or subfolder

1 Open Finder and in the Sidebar click Documents.

2 Control + click to open the contextual menu.

3 Click New Folder.

4 Type the name for the folder.

5 Press Enter on the keyboard.

For your information

To rename the folder (or if you could not type a name in Step 3), click the folder once to select it, press Enter on the keyboard, then type the name. Press Enter again to apply.

4

Manipulate files and folders (cont.)

Move a folder

1. From the Finder, locate the folder to move.

2. Method one:
   a. Drag the folder to the desktop.
   b. From the Finder, locate the area where the moved folder should belong.
   c. Drag the folder there.

3. Method 2:
   a. Drag the folder from its current position to the folder you'd like to put it in.
   b. While holding down the mouse button, wait for the folder to open.
   c. Drop the folder into this folder or any subfolder.

Move a folder

If you create a folder and decide later it should be somewhere else, you can move it. Moving isn't an option from any contextual menu, though (except to move it to the Trash), and with folders there's no option to 'cut' either. Thus, it's good to know a little trick for moving folders that works easily, which you'll learn here.

However, before you start moving folders around, which can have unforeseen consequences, consider creating an alias instead. Aliases are harmless, can be placed anywhere, take up only a minuscule amount of disk space and will act as a shortcut to a folder you've created. It may be in your best interests to leave, say, your Travel Plans folder in Documents but create an alias for it in another folder you've created (perhaps Favorite Activities). You can still use the Travel Plans folder, but you can access it from another Finder window. If you're sure you want to move a folder though, you can!

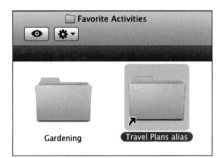

? Did you know?

You can't move system folders.

Rename, copy or delete a folder

As you create folders and subfolders, you may decide you'd like to rename them, copy them or delete them. Renaming a folder so that it better represents its contents is a great idea; deleting entire folders of data that you don't need any more is also a good idea. Some data, such as travel itineraries, to-do lists, etc., outlives its usefulness, and there's no reason for it to continue to take up space on your hard drive or clutter up another folder or the desktop. However, I often suggest users avoid copying data (like folders and files) for many reasons: it's easier and more effective to create an alias, it's difficult to make changes in both places or manage two sets of similar data, and duplicate data takes up extra space on your hard drive.

On a Mac there are often multiple ways to perform a task. You can use a mouse click, a key combination, and often you can drag and drop. You can perform tasks from contextual menus too, accessible from Ctrl + click or a right-click. That said, what is introduced here for renaming, copying and deleting folders is certainly not the only way to do it.

- To rename a folder: click the folder once to select it. Press Enter on the keyboard. Type a new name. Press Enter again.
- To copy a folder: Ctrl + click or right-click and select Copy. (You can now repeat to paste the copied folder wherever you like.)
- Delete a folder: drag the folder to the Trash icon on the Dock.

Copy or move a file

As you know, Copy is an option from most contextual menus. Move is not. You'll copy and move files the same way you copy and move folders, though. Remember, copying creates a duplicate, something you probably don't want. Moving actually moves the file to a new place. To copy or move a file:

- Ctrl + click or right-click and select Copy. Repeat the process to paste. Note you can also select Duplicate and then drag the duplicate file to the desired location.
- To move a file – Drag the file to the desktop, then drag it to the appropriate area using the Finder.

!

Important

When you delete a folder you delete everything in it, too!

?

Did you know?

Even after deleting a folder, file or other piece of data, you can still recover it from the Trash (provided you haven't yet emptied the Trash).

4

Manipulate files and folders (cont.)

Compress a folder of data

1. Locate the folder to compress.

2. Ctrl + click or right-click and choose Compress <name>.

3. Note the newly compressed folder.

4. If desired, drag the original file to the Trash.

5. When you need the data again, double-click the compressed file to open it.

Rename or delete a file

You can rename a file and delete a file using the same techniques you learned earlier to rename and delete folders. For some variety, here are two additional techniques to try.

- To rename a file: click Ctrl + click or right-click and choose Get Info. Under Name & Extensions, type a new name.

- To delete a file: Ctrl + click or right-click, and from the contextual menu that appears, click Move to Trash.

Compress a file or folder

You can compress files and folders to make them smaller and cause them to take up less space on your hard drive. Compressing files and folders is generally done only for data that you plan to store long term, and isn't generally applied to all the data on your computer or to data you access regularly. Compression is most commonly used when it's applied to data prior to sending it in an email, before uploading it to an FTP site, or before sharing it using a similar method. Compressing data before sending it helps the data get to the recipient faster than if it were not compressed, and compressing data before storing it for the long term on an external hard drive, DVD or network drive helps save space on the drive for additional data.

However robust a computer and its operating system, it's always possible for the system to crash or for data to be lost. There are many ways this can happen. You can lose data through no fault of your own: your computer could be lost or stolen, or you could have a fire or a flood. The electricity could go out just as you're finishing a large presentation for your boss, perhaps causing a corrupted file that can't be opened. You could inadvertently delete a cherished photo or a necessary program file. Your computer could get a virus. Because there are so many ways data loss can occur, you should be prepared. You need to create a backup strategy, set it up and play a role in making sure that data is backed up regularly. If you have Lion, you should be aware of the new Auto Save Resume and Versions features.

Save, back up and recover files and folders

4

Use Lion's new Auto Save features

Lion comes with three unique features that aren't available in earlier OS X versions. They are Resume, Auto Save and Versions. You can use these features to pick up where you left off should there be a power cut, a restart caused by a software update, or some similar interruption. They give you more control over your work should you make changes and save them and then change your mind.

Resume

Resume is a feature you use with apps. (You get apps from the App Store, which was introduced in Chapter 2.) You use apps to perform tasks, including but not limited to calculations, playing games, keeping track of workouts or calories, even converting files from one type to another. It used to be that if you were in an app and you had to restart your computer, you had to start from scratch with the app. With Resume, apps you close will reopen exactly where you left off – a nifty new feature! With Resume, you can restart your Mac and return to what you were doing and find all your apps just where you left them.

Auto Save

You may be familiar with the mantra 'save early and save often'. You may be in the habit of doing that already. That's great, but if you ever forget, Auto Save is here to help. Auto Save saves your work periodically, even if you forget to. Auto Save is what makes another new feature, Versions, work. With Auto Save and Versions you can access your file in various stages of development. You can also click File>Save a Version if you want to save a file in its current condition, thinking you may want to revert to it later.

But why 'save a version'? Here's a common scenario. You open a file, make changes, click Save, close the program and log off your machine or shut it down. Then you realise you have made a huge mistake and you need to undo all those changes. Without Versions, those changes are permanent. With Versions, and by saving your own versions at optimal moments, you can keep this from happening in the future. Interested? Read on!

Versions

You've edited documents before, so you know that a document can go through lots of changes as it's being created and before it's finalised. You also know that Auto Save creates various versions of files as you work, saving changes automatically so you don't have to. OS X Lion automatically creates a new version of a document each time you open it and every hour while you're working on it, too. And you can create a version yourself, from the File menu.

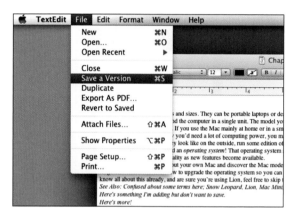

As these versions are created, you may wonder how you can revert to one or even manage your options. It's easy: just click File and click Revert to Saved. Then look at the versions and pick the one you want to use and click Restore (or Done). You can also copy and paste between versions. Of course, you can simply ignore all of this and work as you've always worked, especially if this all seems a bit over the top to you.

For your information

When you share a document with someone, you share only the most recent copy, not all the hard work it took to get there.

4

Back up data with Time Machine

Time Machine is an application included with your Mac that lets you back up your data automatically. Time Machine keeps hourly backups for the past 24 hours, daily backups for the past month, and weekly backups for the previous months until the disk you're using to back up to is full. Then it writes over the oldest backups. You have to enable and set up Time Machine for it to work. You also need an external drive to save the backup to. For Time Machine to work properly, make sure you get a large external drive (160 GB or more). Once you have the drive, connect it and let it install. Then you can set up Time Machine.

Set up Time Machine

1 Click System Preferences on the Dock or open it from the Applications folder.

2 Under System, click Time Machine.

3 Move the slider from Off to On. (You may have to click the lock in the bottom left corner first.)

4 Choose the external drive from the list of drives when prompted. (If you aren't prompted, click Select Disk.)

5 Click the disk and then click Use for Backup.

6 Click Options and configure options as desired.

7 A backup will occur automatically.

Time Machine

OFF / ON

Important

If prompted to erase what's currently on the drive, create a backup of it first on another computer if possible, or choose another backup device.

Did you know?

You can secure your hard drive by encrypting its contents. A password must be entered to decrypt the data, which protects your data from thieves and hackers. You do this using FileVault, an option in System Preferences, under Security. FileVault secures your home folder and it is automatically encrypted and decrypted while you're using it.

Use built-in applications, utilities and apps from the App Store

5

Introduction

Lots of applications come preinstalled on your Mac. The applications you have access to let you perform tasks, obtain media, send email and surf the Web, among other things. You can install your own applications, too – you may have opted to purchase and install iWork, for instance, or software that came with a printer or scanner. You've probably already used a few of the built-in applications, perhaps Safari to surf the Web.

In addition to applications, your Mac offers utilities. Utilities help you perform system tasks, such as migrating computer settings and data from your old computer to your new one, getting information about your Mac like how much RAM or hard drive space you have, and fixing problems with your hard disk, including problems involving permissions for files, among other things. You won't use the utilities nearly as often as you use applications. In fact, you may never use them.

Finally, there are apps. Apps are applications you get from the App Store. These can be just about anything, as you've learned already. You might get a simple game that lets you fling birds into stacked objects (for only a few pounds), or you might opt for a fully-fledged program like Final Cut Pro X (which is much more expensive and complex). You can upgrade to Lion through the App Store, too.

What you'll do

Find and open an application

Use a simple application

Find and explore Utilities

Use a simple utility

Open and explore the App Store

Purchase and download an app

Locate and use an app

Explore full-screen apps

In this chapter you'll learn how to access, open and use some of the applications that come with your Mac. You'll learn how to locate utilities and know what's available should you need them. Finally, you'll use the App Store to purchase an app, then use Launchpad in Lion to access it.

Important

Up to now I've been including detailed instructions for both Lion and pre-Lion OSes. From here on, I'll be discussing Lion only. If you don't have Lion yet, consider upgrading. If you don't want Lion, you can still use this book effectively: just ignore any Lion-specific features and understand that some of the screen shots you see here won't match what's on your computer (what you find in the sidebar of Finder and on the Dock, for instance).

You've seen the Applications folder in previous chapters. You can access this folder from the Dock (provided you haven't moved it) and from the Finder window. You can also search for a specific application from any Spotlight Search window. Here is the Applications folder as shown from the Dock; it's configured to appear by Name, by Folder and by Grid (you can right-click the Applications folder on the Dock to configure yours to look like this, if you wish). If you use the window shown here, make sure you note the scroll bars – they blend in with the window itself and can be easily missed. You'll use the scroll bars to access applications that won't fit in the window.

The items contained in the Applications window are the applications installed on your Mac. They include the built-in applications such as Address Book, App Store, Calculator, Chess, and so on, as well as applications you've installed, perhaps an anti-virus program, Microsoft Office, or a game. You can access apps from the App Store here, too. There's an alternative to the Applications window if you use Lion – it's called Launchpad. Whatever route you take to get to an application, you open it by either clicking it once or by double-clicking, depending on the circumstances.

◀ Explore Applications

Open and explore applications

1 Open the Finder.

2 Click Applications.

3 Maximise the window and/or use the scroll bars as necessary to view the applications.

4 If desired, change the view so that the application icons appear as thumbnails, in lists or in another view.

!

Important

If you don't see the Applications folder on the Dock and you want it there, open the Finder, click Applications, then drag it to the right end of the Dock, to the left of the Trash. Once there, right-click it and configure the options for viewing it.

5

Explore Applications (cont.)

If you don't have a lot of experience with applications, you may want to start by exploring some of the simpler ones. Calculator is intuitive and easy to use, as are Chess, Dictionary and Safari. You might also try Stickies (for creating your own sticky notes) or TextEdit for writing simple letters. Once you're familiar with the less complicated apps, using others will come more easily.

Make a note with Stickies

1. From the Finder's Application window, open Stickies. Read what's on offer.

2. Verify Stickies is showing on the menu bar and click File>New Note.

3. Type your note.

4. Click Font>Show Fonts. If desired, choose a new Font Size.

5. To quit Stickies, click Stickies>Quit Stickies.

Play a game of Chess

1. In the Finder, click Applications.

2. Click Chess.

3. Use your mouse to click and drag a chess piece to play it.

4. Wait while your Mac makes a move.

5. In between moves, take time to explore the menu bar options.

See also

Learn more about Launchpad in Chapter 2.

Did you know?

You can drag any application's icon to the desktop (or anywhere else) to create an alias for it there.

While you'll find yourself in the Applications folder or Applications window quite often, you'll rarely find yourself inside the Utilities folder. For the most part, barring a few unique applications, what's in the Utilities folder is strictly for configuring and troubleshooting system features. For instance, you can use Activity Monitor to see how hard your computer's processor (CPU) is working, the AirPort Utility to find other AirPort wireless devices on your network, the Network Utility to display information about your network including highly technical things like routing table information and network statistics, and so on. The Utilities folder is inside the Applications folder and contains the items shown here.

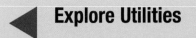

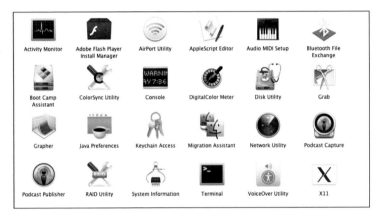

As noted, there are a few items in the Utilities folder you'll find interesting and may use regularly (or at least on occasion). They are:

- Bluetooth File Exchange – with this utility you can select a file to send to another Bluetooth device that is turned on, synced and nearby. You may use this utility to send a file to a device such as an iPhone or iPad, for instance.

- Grab – this utility doesn't seem to do anything after opening it, but you will see the menu bar change. With Grab, you can capture a screen shot of a selection, a window or the entire screen, and you can even take a timed shot. You can then share this screen shot with others. Refer to the panel to learn how to use this utility.

- VoiceOver Utility – you'll use this to configure VoiceOver, a utility that can read what's on the screen to you.

For your information

If you've opened several applications and utilities, you'll see their icons on the Dock. Control + click and select Quit to close them (and remove them from the Dock).

5

Explore Utilities (cont.)

🍎	**Grab**	File	Edit	Capture	Window	Help
				Selection	⇧⌘A	
				Window	⇧⌘W	
				Screen	⌘Z	
				Timed Screen	⇧⌘Z	

Take a screen shot with the Grab utility

1 Open Applications and open Utilities.

2 Open Grab.

3 Notice the menu bar now offers Grab options.

4 Click Capture and click Selection. (Note the other options.)

5 Use your mouse to drag to select a particular part of the screen, perhaps part of the Utilities window, or choose a window if prompted (by clicking it).

6 To save the screen capture that appears, from the menu bar click File>Save and complete the saving process. You can also print or duplicate.

Important

!

You can easily lose the Grab menu bar options. They will disappear if another application or window becomes active. To access the Grab menu options again, click Grab on the Dock.

The App Store is a store where you can get apps (applications). To use the App Store you need to have set up an Apple ID, which you've probably done. If you haven't, though, don't worry, you'll be prompted if need be. The App Store icon is on the Dock, but if you've moved it you can also find it in the Applications folder or in the Finder.

The App Store contains several tabs that run across the top and various quick links on the right side. In the body of the interface are apps that relate to whatever you've selected in the sorting fields. For instance, if you click Top Charts on the top of the App Store interface and News on the right (under Top Charts Categories), the apps you'll see will all be news-related and will include listings of Top Paid, Top Free and Top Grossing.

◀ Explore the App Store

Explore the App Store tabs

1 Open the App Store.

2 Review what's shown under the Featured tab, then click Top Charts.

3 Explore what's shown under Top Charts and click Categories.

4 Repeat with the other tab titles.

ⓘ For your information

If you're having trouble scrolling with a mouse or trackpad, try scrolling in the opposite direction to the one you're used to. Lion has changed the rules with regard to scrolling.

5

Explore the App Store (cont.)

Get a free game from the App Store

1 From the Finder's Application window, open the App Store.

2 At the top of the App Store window, click Top Charts.

3 In the right pane, under Top Charts Categories, click Games.

4 Locate Top Free.

5 Locate a free game you'd like to play and click Free, then Install App. (Note that you can click See All next to Top Free Games to see more games.)

6 Type your Apple ID and/or password and click Sign In.

7 Watch the app install in Launchpad, which opens automatically.

Did you know? **?**

You can use the arrow keys on the keyboard to scroll up and down in a window

---

The tabs you'll explore include:

- Featured – these are apps that Apple deems new and noteworthy, 'hot', or are considered staff favourites.

- Top Charts – these are apps that are the most popular and have been downloaded the most. They are separated into Top Paid, Top Free and Top Grossing.

- Categories – here, a list of categories is available. Categories include Business, Education, Finance, Games, etc. If you know what kind of app you want, this is the place to look.

- Purchased – here you'll find a list of apps you've purchased. If you've moved an app to the Trash and decide you want it again, Installed will become Install, allowing you to install the app again should you change your mind.

- Updates – you won't see anything under this tab until updates become available for an app you've purchased (or downloaded for free) from the App Store.

For your information **i**

If you can't see the scroll bars in the App Store window, one way to make them appear is to resize the window just a little, by dragging from the right side. However, you can use your mouse to scroll up and down using the scroll wheel or the arrows on the keyboard, even if those scroll bars are hidden on the screen.

Once you've downloaded and installed something from the App Store, you can open it and use it. In Lion, you can locate the app in the Applications window or you can use Launchpad. Launchpad is generally on the Dock and its icon looks like a rocket ship.

As with any application, you simply click (or double-click) an app's icon to open it. The first time you use an app you may see directions, be prompted to type your name, or you may be prompted to do something else such as enable location services or allow notifications. Almost all apps offer a way to configure preferences, too. Even this Solitaire game offers options to mute sounds, disable score display, enable and disable hints, change the wallpaper, and choose from a long list of card games (shown here). You can explore whichever app you're using from the menu bar and from inside the app itself.

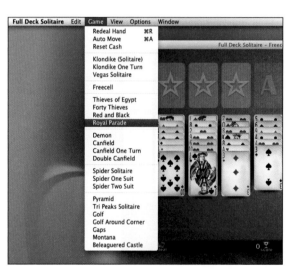

◀ **Locate and use apps**

Open Launchpad and use an app

1 Open Launchpad from the Dock or the Finder's Application window.

2 Locate the game you downloaded in the previous section and open it, or choose any other app you've downloaded.

3 Read any introductory materials.

4 Review the options under the menus on the menu bar.

5 Explore the app's interface until you're ready to play or use the app.

5

?

Did you know?

You probably have more apps than will fit on a single screen. Use the arrows on the keyboard, flick left and right with a trackpad, or use your mouse to click the dots at the bottom of Launchpad to explore other screens. You can even click and drag the mouse across the screen to move among Launchpad screens.

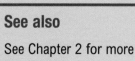

See also

See Chapter 2 for more information about Launchpad.

Use Safari, Mail, iCal and Address Book

Introduction

Safari and Mail both come preinstalled with your Mac and both require a connection to the Internet. There are lots of ways to connect to the Internet, including through a dial-up modem, cable modem, DSL modem or via satellite service. One popular option is to connect to an existing network in your home or business using either Wi-Fi or Ethernet. Another is to connect through a free Wi-Fi hotspot such as the ones you'll find in coffee shops, hotel lobbies or libraries. (You'll need a laptop you can take there to do that, though.) Once you're connected to the Internet, you'll be ready to use Safari to surf the Web and Mail to retrieve, send and manage your email.

After you've spent some time with Safari and Mail, you can start to incorporate other applications that complement these. Two that integrate nicely are iCal and Address Book, both available by default on the Dock. iCal is a calendar application that you use to enter events and set reminders, and you can share these events with others using Mail, perhaps to invite them to events you create. Address Book is an application that enables you to maintain and organise the information about the people you contact, and offers a place to input their email address, phone number, street address and similar data. Once you've entered a contact in the Address Book, you can access it from Mail and iCal, among other places.

See also

Chapter 7 covers networking, including how to connect to an existing network, such as one you'd find in your home, a business, or a public place such as a pub or coffee house.

What you'll do

Visit a web page

Explore Thumbnail view

Learn how to download a program

Create bookmarks and bookmark folders

Configure tabbed browsing

Use Safari Reader

Set up your email accounts in Mail

Receive, reply to, forward and compose email

Attach a file or insert a picture

Open attachments

Minimise spam

Customise Mail

Explore Lion-specific features of Mail

Create an iCal event and share it

Use Address Book to manage contacts

Surf the Web with Safari

The World Wide Web (the Web, the net, or the Internet to you and me) has become such a part of our everyday experience that it's difficult to imagine life without it. Anything and everything you can think of (and probably a lot you can't!) has a web page devoted to it. You can shop online, indulge your hobbies with likeminded people, acquire academic qualifications via distance learning courses, watch movies, listen to the radio, download music and watch homemade videos. Frankly, it would be easier to list what you can't do than what you can! You experience the Web through a web 'browser'. In the case of the Mac, that's Safari.

Explore the Safari interface

When you open Safari for the first time, you'll probably be taken to Apple's home page. You can quickly jump to other web pages, though, and you can easily search for information on any topic from the search window. You'll find Safari on the Dock. If you don't see the Safari icon on the Dock, search for it from the menu bar (click the magnifying glass and type Safari).

When you open Safari you'll see various items included in its interface. These features help you use Safari effectively. Here are a few to look for:

a. Minimise Safari

b. Back and Forward buttons

c. Bookmarks bar

d. Thumbnail view

e. Address bar

f. Search window

g. Add Bookmark icon

h. Refresh

i. Reader

j. Drop-down lists

The new, faster
MacBook Air

The ultimate everyday notebook.
Now up to 2.5x faster, featuring high-speed
Thunderbolt I/O and OS X Lion.

Open and explore Safari

1 From the Dock, open Safari.

2 Locate the items and features highlighted in the screen shot.

3 Note the menu bar (not shown). Click Safari and click Preferences.

4 Explore the preferences as time allows.

5 Close the Preferences window.

6 Type *www.google.com* in the Address bar.

7 Press Enter on the keyboard.

For your information

You won't see Reader if you're using a pre-Lion OS.

Did you know?

If Safari is not on the Dock and you want it there, open the Finder, click Applications and drag Safari from the Applications window to the Dock. (Safari will still be available from the Applications window.)

Surf the Web
with Safari
(cont.)

View thumbnails of websites

1 Click the thumbnails icon in Safari.

2 Verify Top Sites is selected.

3 Click any site to go there.

4 Click the thumbnails icon again.

5 Click History.

6 Click any web page, and click it again to go there.

The first thing you'll do when you use Safari is to type in a web address (such as *www.google.com*) or click a link to go to a web page. You might also access pages from any bookmark lists or one of the preconfigured items on the Bookmarks bar. When you move from page to page and explore the Web (in any manner), it's called 'surfing' the Internet. If you're just starting to explore Safari and the Web, this is a good way to familiarise yourself with what's available.

Sometimes you'll want to search for information on a particular topic instead of blindly clicking links, perhaps to find the latest score in a football match or to get directions to a new restaurant you've heard about. As you search, try to be aware of where you're heading off to before you click a link. For instance, when browsing a list of results, look at the name of the link under the summary of what the page offers. If the link leads back to a website you trust, such as Google, Amazon or Yahoo, the results are more likely to be reliable and less likely to lead you to something you don't want to see (such as pornography or an advertisement). Remember too that you can't believe everything you read: just because it's on the Internet by no means makes it true!

If you aren't sure what you want to do on the Web, or you aren't sure where to start, Safari offers a really nice jumping-off point. It's called Thumbnail view. The icon is on the Bookmarks bar and it looks like a set of small squares. Click this view to see what Apple deems Top Sites. You can also access pages you've recently visited by clicking the History button. As you surf the Web, what you see in Top Sites will change, depending on the pages you visit most often.

As you surf the Web you'll run across things you want to have on your computer. These may be audiobooks, music files, PDF documents, videos, movies, apps, wallpapers or even programs. The safest way to obtain these is from the App Store, detailed in Chapter 5, and through iTunes, detailed in Chapter 9. However, sometimes what you want won't be available in either of these places. Perhaps you want to download an audiobook from Audible, or maybe you're prompted to download and install something to make a website work properly, like Flash Player.

Although I will heartily suggest you stay away from most downloads from places other than the App Store and iTunes, there are programs you'll need from third-party websites and they are safe to download. For instance, you might need Adobe Reader to read certain types of documents, and if you get it from *www.adobe.com*, you'll be OK. You may want to purchase something like an anti-virus program from a site that's not Apple-related; again, a safe move if you get the software from a trusted e-tailer.

It's important to make the distinction that downloading something and installing it are two separate things. Some people download a file or program and then wonder where it's gone. This is especially true in the age of the App Store and iTunes because once you buy something from there, it's downloaded, it installs and it's ready without further intervention. That's not the way it works for the rest of the Internet.

In the 'real world', downloading is the process of copying the data necessary from the web onto your computer. That data is often the required installation files, a document, a book or something similar. Once a download is complete, if the item you've downloaded is an application, you must still install it. The installation files will appear in the Downloads folder. You'll click the download to start the installation process. If the downloaded item is a book or file, you must click it to open it – it won't open automatically.

Download and install a program

6

! Important

It's often difficult to know whether a download is safe or not. It's also often difficult to get the 'free' version of something without downloading spyware or adware along with it or getting hoodwinked into paying for it later. The best way to find out whether a download is safe and worthy of disk space is to read reviews and search the Internet for user comments and complaints.

Download and install a program (cont.)

To understand how downloading and installing works in places other than the App Store and iTunes, work through the steps here to download and install Flash Player. You'll need it and it's a great way to learn how the process works.

Download Flash Player

1 Use Safari to navigate to *http://get.adobe.com/ flashplayer*.

2 Select your operating system and version, then click Download now.

3 Click the Install option. You may see this option in more than one place.

4 When presented with the warning box, click Open to continue.

5 If applicable, perform any preinstallation tasks, such as agreeing to Terms of Service.

6 Click Install.

7 Type your password and click OK.

8 Wait while the program installs.

Important !

You may be prompted to close related programs before installing a program. If so, click the title bar of the application to make it active, then from the menu bar quit the application.

Did you know? ?

Safari in Lion is an application you can view in 'full-screen mode'. Try it out – hold down these three keys: Control + Apple + F (on a Windows keyboard use Control + Windows + F). Click these again to exit full-screen mode. You can also access the full-screen option in the top right corner of Safari, pressing Esc on the keyboard to exit.

There will be some web pages you'll visit often, perhaps Facebook, a local news website, or a fan page for your favourite football team. You can use Thumbnail view to access them (Top Sites changes as it learns which pages you visit most), or you can bookmark those pages. When you bookmark a page, it will be available in the Bookmarks list, on the Bookmarks bar or in a folder you select or create in either place, depending on how and where you create it. You can then access those pages quickly later, simply by clicking the bookmark you've created.

The first step to creating a bookmark is to navigate to the desired web page. Then, click the + sign on the left side of the Address bar. With that done, you only have to decide where to save the bookmark. You have several choices:

- Reading List – save pages here that contain information you'd like to read later. You can access them by clicking the eyeglasses icon, also shown in the image below on the far left.

- Top Sites – choose this option to add the page to the Top Sites entries in Thumbnail view.

- Bookmarks Bar – choose this entry to save the bookmark to the Bookmarks bar. If there are folders on the Bookmarks bar (such as News and Popular, shown here) and you want the bookmark to be saved to one of them, click it to add the site to the folder.

- Bookmarks Menu – choose this to add the bookmark to the Bookmarks menu. You'll have to click Bookmarks from the menu bar or click the Bookmarks icon to access the items you save here.

For your information ⓘ

I keep bookmarks for pages I visit regularly on the Bookmarks bar. That's the bar that appears just below the Address window. That way, I can revisit a page with a single click. I've also left a few of Apple's default folders there, including News and Popular, because they contain sites I visit often too.

Create bookmarks and bookmark folders (cont.)

Save a bookmark

1. Navigate to a web page you'd like to bookmark.
2. Click the + sign to the left of the Address bar.
3. Select a place for the bookmark.
4. If prompted, type a name for the bookmark or keep the one provided.
5. If applicable, click Add.

I know you'll collect bookmarks. As you collect them, they will start to become unorganised. Thus, it's best to get organised now in preparation for what you'll amass over the lifetime of your Mac. You can start by thinking about the kinds of bookmarks you'll keep and then create folders to represent them. You might create folders named Travel, Health and Reference, for instance. Once you've created these folders, you can start adding websites to them. You can also move existing bookmarks into them.

Important

You can choose bookmark menu from the drop-down list in Step 4, but if you make that a habit your bookmarks list will eventually become cluttered. It's best to create your own bookmark folders, detailed next, and save your bookmarks in them. If you like, you can create folders for the bookmark menu and the Bookmarks bar.

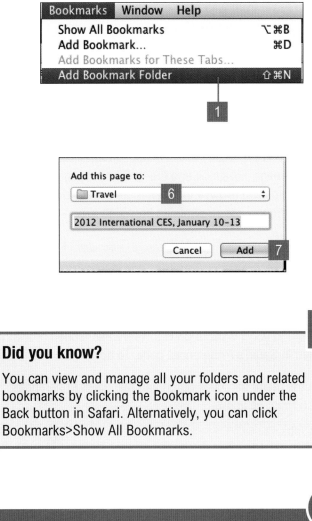

Create a bookmark folder

1 With Safari open and active, from the menu bar click Bookmarks and Add Bookmark Folder.

2 Type a name for the folder. I created a folder called Travel.

3 Repeat to add all of the desired folders. (You can drag the new folder to the Bookmarks bar if you like.)

4 Browse to any web page to bookmark.

5 Click the + sign to add a bookmark.

6 Choose the appropriate folder to hold the bookmark.

7 Click Add.

Did you know?

You can view and manage all your folders and related bookmarks by clicking the Bookmark icon under the Back button in Safari. Alternatively, you can click Bookmarks>Show All Bookmarks.

For your information

Beside the Bookmarks menu on the menu bar is History. Click the History menu to show sites you've recently visited, to reopen all windows from your last session, to clear your history list, and more.

Configure and use tabbed browsing

When you move from web page to web page on the Internet, you lose the page you're on and a new page appears in its place. With this method, in order to have two web pages open at one time you'd need to open Safari twice and thus you'd have two Safari windows open on the screen. You can have more than one web page open at a time in only one Safari window by integrating tabbed browsing. Once multiple tabs are open you can click the tab to go to the page while leaving the other pages open and available. Here, I've opened three tabs: the Apple home page, Facebook and the BBC home page. Tabbed browsing helps you browse the Web more effectively and makes for an altogether more streamlined browsing experience.

The first thing you'll want to do is to verify that tabbed browsing is enabled in Safari's Preferences pane. To do this:

1. From the menu bar, click Safari and then click Preferences. (Safari must be active.)

2. Click Tabs.

3. Choose Open pages in tabs instead of windows: Automatically.

4. Tick When a new tab or window opens, make it active.

With that done, you're ready to start using tabs. Try these techniques for using tabbed browsing:

- Hold down the Apple key (or Windows key) while you click on a link to open the link in a new tab and make that tab active.

- Hold down the Apple key (or Windows key) + Shift + click on a link to open the link in a new tab. The page you're on will remain the active tab.

- Hold down the Apple (or Windows) key + Option (or Alt) + click a link to open the link in a new Safari window. When you do this, you'll have two Safari windows open.

Another way to incorporate tabbed browsing is to open all your favourite web pages and bookmark them all in a single folder. You can save this folder to the Bookmarks bar. Then with a single click you can open all the pages in their own tabs at one time.

Add this bookmarks folder to:
📖 Bookmarks Bar ⬢ 4 ⬍
My Favorite Web Pages
Cancel · Add · 5

Did you know?

If you want Safari to open to the same web page every time you open it, navigate to the page, then click Safari, Preferences, and from the General tab next to Homepage, click Set to Current Page.

Configure and use tabbed browsing (cont.)

6

Configure a group of bookmarks

1 Using what you know about tabbed browsing, open your four or five favourite web pages.

2 Click Bookmarks on the menu bar.

3 Click Add Bookmarks for These ___ Tabs.

4 Verify Bookmarks Bar is selected and type a name for the new group.

5 Click Add.

6 Now any time you want to open all these pages at the same time, click the bookmark you created on the Bookmarks bar.

Use Safari Reader

Sometimes, when you come across an article you want to read, the elements included with the article distract you from the article's message. If you have a visual impairment or if you use VoiceOver when surfing the Web (and it tries to read these elements), problems can crop up. It's certainly easier to read an article when you can just get to the text and ignore the rest, even if you don't have a visual impairment or reading disability. If you find yourself in a position where elements in an article cause a distraction, keep an eye out for the Reader icon in Safari's Address bar. If you see it, you can click it to view the article without many of the diverting elements.

Use Safari Reader

1. Visit *www.Wikipedia.com*.

2. Browse the articles by clicking links on any page.

3. When you see Reader in the Address bar, click it.

4. Use the controls to zoom in or out as desired, to email the page or to print it, or to close the Reader window.

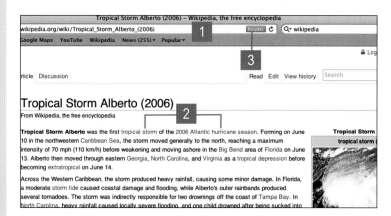

For your information ⓘ

If you want to print an article you find on the Web and Reader is an option, click it and print from the Reader. Many of the elements you won't want to print, such as the ads, will be removed.

For your information ⓘ

If the controls disappear, position your mouse at the bottom of the Reader page. They'll appear again.

Although I haven't discussed everything there is to know about Safari, you know enough now to continue experimenting. Go ahead and click all the items on the menu bar and click the icons on Safari's interface. Try key combinations such as Shift + click (on a link) and Control + click on a link. You'll discover lots of keyboard shortcuts this way.

You have two main options for accessing your email from your Mac. You can log on to your email provider's website using Safari or you can set up and use Mail. I prefer Mail to Safari because it's easy to save and organise email, include pictures and attach other data to outgoing mail, and review what you've sent and saved. You can also manage several email accounts from a single interface, so there's no back and forth when you need to check multiple mail accounts. Mail also integrates nicely with iCal (a calendar application) and Address Book (a contact-management application), both also included with your Mac. You'll learn a little about both of these towards the end of the chapter.

When you first open Mail, you'll be prompted to set it up. Mail doesn't yet know which email address(es) you use, which ISP you use or which passwords you've chosen. Thus when you open it for the first time you'll see a Welcome to Mail screen and two buttons: one to quit and one to continue. Of course, you'll click Continue!

There are really only two types of mail accounts you'll want to set up, although there are more types available than those I'll detail here. For the most part, you'll have either a web-based email account from an entity such as Google or Apple, or you'll have an email account from an ISP, such as BT.

Web-based email accounts are pretty easy to set up; email accounts from ISPs take a little more work.

For your information

If you need an email address, consider one from Gmail. It integrates nicely with Mail, it's free, you can access your email from anywhere (even your smart phone) and it is easy to set up.

Set up Mail (cont.)

Set up a Web-based email account

1 Open Mail. If prompted to set up an account skip to Step 3.

2 If you aren't prompted to set up an account or want to set up a second account, click File>Add Account.

3 Type or accept your name and type your email address and password.

4 Click Create.

5 If Mail can configure the account automatically, click Create. Otherwise, you'll have to input additional information (refer to the panel on p. 99).

6 You'll be able to see easily when you have new email from the Dock.

If you input the basic information about your email address and your account is configured automatically, you're ready to use Mail with that account. Mail can set up many accounts automatically because it knows the settings, mail server names, port numbers and other technical information and can input it for you, behind the scenes, for well-known, public email entities. If, after inputting your email address and password, you're prompted for additional information, it's because Mail *can't* configure it automatically. This happens because different ISPs use different mail 'servers' for receiving and distributing email that's sent to you, and for sending out emails you compose, and those mail servers have to be input into Mail. These ISPs may also require you to log on with some sort of secure authentication, use a specific port, and so on. You may also have to set up an account manually if Mail can't send your password securely to a server that requires it.

During manual set-up you may see the following options or terms:

- Description – you can type anything here. Generally, you'll type the name of your ISP if you have more than one email account to configure.

- Mail server – this is the mail server your ISP uses to send email and receive it; you'll have an incoming server and an outgoing server. You'll have to enter two mail server names (one for each). You'll have to ask your ISP for this information and type it exactly.

- User name – this is almost always your email address, but sometimes it isn't. Call your ISP to find out.

- Secure Sockets Layer – also called SSL, this is a secure authentication method for logging on to your account. Most of the time your password is your authentication credential.

- IMAP – Internet Message Access Protocol, used to access email messages from the Web.

- POP – Post Office Protocol, a system by which emails are retrieved from remote servers (i.e. Mail connects to your ISP's POP server and collects your email).

- RSS – Really Simple Syndication, a format for distributing frequently updated web content such as news headlines, podcasts and blogs.

- SMTP – Simple Mail Transfer Protocol, the email-sending counterpart to POP. It's the outgoing server.

Input additional information when warranted

1. If prompted during account set-up, click Setup Manually.

2. Leave POP selected unless you're positive you need to select something else.

3. Fill in the required information. You may well have to contact your ISP.

4. Click Continue.

5. Continue working through the screens offered. What you see and input will differ depending on your email provider's requirements.

! Important

Some email providers require you to enable various security features during account creation. If you encounter any problems, call your ISP for help or search for the proper settings on the Web.

Set up Mail (cont.)

When you have to set up an email account manually, you may encounter problems. While it may seem to flow smoothly during the creation process, once you try to get your mail, or send mail, something often goes wrong. You get errors. When this happens you'll have to review your settings for that account. To access the current settings and make changes:

1. Click Mail, then click Preferences.

2. Click the account in the left pane if more than one exist and click the Account Information tab.

3. Call your ISP or look up the settings on the Internet.

4. Replace the incorrect information with the correct information.

5. Click the Advanced tab.

6. Review this information too. If applicable, replace any incorrect settings with the settings your ISP requires.

Did you know?

You can disable an account from Mail's Preferences pane. Click the account in the left pane and click Advanced. Then deselect Enable this account.

Once your account is set up correctly, email will arrive automatically. Don't be alarmed if 100+ emails appear! Mail may download email you've already seen on your mobile device or on another computer, even if you've deleted it. An ISP's mail servers will often keep a week's worth of emails available and they may appear here when you set up Mail. (Alternatively, perhaps no mail will appear!)

Once Mail is open, explore the interface. One thing to explore is the ability to view Mail in full-screen mode. Click the double arrows in the top right corner to engage it; click Esc on the keyboard to restore the view.

The next thing to explore is the Show button. Click it to show the navigation pane. When you click Show, it becomes Hide (which is what you see in the screen shot below). Now you'll have access to all your email account mailboxes if you have set up more than one account, and you can pick a single account as shown here. You can also access folders such as Sent, Trash, RSS feeds and others you may have created with your web-based accounts. You can see the folders I created in Gmail, School and Travel.

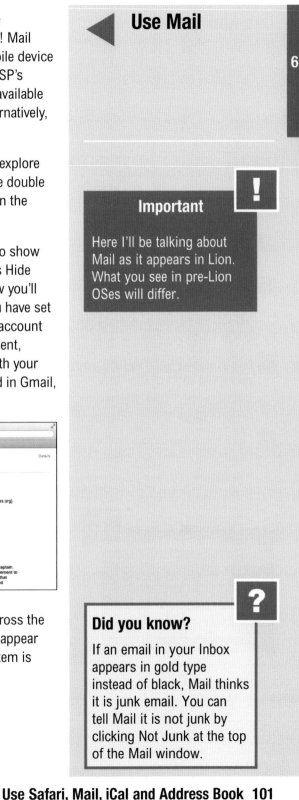

Important !

Here I'll be talking about Mail as it appears in Lion. What you see in pre-Lion OSes will differ.

Finally, hover your mouse over every icon that runs across the top of Mail's interface. When you hover, a pop-up will appear giving you a brief explanation of what that particular item is used for.

Did you know? ?

If an email in your Inbox appears in gold type instead of black, Mail thinks it is junk email. You can tell Mail it is not junk by clicking Not Junk at the top of the Mail window.

Use Mail (cont.)

Reply to and forward email

1. Click any email to reply to or forward.

2. Click the icon for Reply, Reply All or Forward.

3. If you clicked Forward in Step 3, type the address of the person you'd like to forward the email to.

4. If applicable, remove any unwanted parts of the email or type a few sentences in the body of the email.

5. Type your response and click Send. The Send icon looks like a paper aeroplane.

Receive, reply to, forward and compose email

The icons that run across the top of Mail's interface (shown on the previous page) are the tools you'll use most often. For instance, the icon that looks like an envelope is where you'll click to check for new messages. The one next to it, which looks like a piece of paper and a pencil, is what you'll click to compose a new email message. If you continue down the line until you get to the left-facing arrow, that's the icon to click to reply to the sender of a selected message. The icon next to that is Reply to All. Finally, the right-facing arrow is where you'll click to forward a selected email to someone else. Although there are others (including one to create a simple note and another to flag a specific message with colour), these are the icons you'll use most.

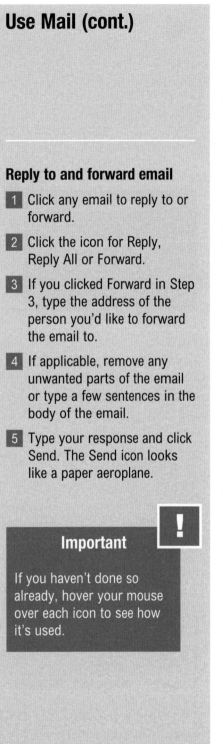

Although the icons may look different from any you've used before, what you already know about email in other programs or on mobile devices applies in Mail. When you click Reply, for instance, if the email was sent to you as well as to others you'll reply only to the sender. If you click Reply to All, your response will go to everyone. If you click Forward, you'll type in a new email address to send the email to. Nothing has changed and there's nothing new to learn here, except which icon to use to do what.

? Did you know?

You can click the icon to retrieve your email any time for Mail to see whether new mail has arrived at your ISP. Otherwise, Mail will automatically check for mail every 5 minutes.

On a similar note, when you compose a new email, you can choose which email address to send from if you have more than one configured, you can add pictures and attach files, and you can use various fonts and formatting during the composition of your email. Of course, you can apply formatting and such to replies and forwards, but for the most part you'll use these special features when you compose an email from scratch.

The new message window will look somewhat different from what you've seen before. It will also contain features you aren't familiar with. Open a new message window (click the Compose New Mail icon) and explore the icons outlined next to see what I mean.

In any new message window, you have access to additional icons that are related only to composing a new email:

- The paperclip icon is for attaching files, pictures and other data.

- The Font icon (A) is for showing and hiding the format bar, where you can access formatting options such as font, font size, font colour, bold, italic and underline, justification options, bullets and numbering, and more. Overleaf the format bar is showing.

- The Photo Browser icon is used to show or hide the photo browser window. When this window is open you can drag photos from it to your email.

- The Stationery pane icon can be used to show and hide stationery options. There's stationery for birthdays, announcements, photos, sentiments and more. When you choose a stationery for a background, you can type right on top of it. Here I've selected the 'Sticky' stationery.

?

Did you know?

When you compose an email, you can attach something to it. Often this will be a picture or a document, but it could be a short video or music file, too. You don't have to attach anything, though; you can simply create a new email composed of text.

Use Mail (cont.)

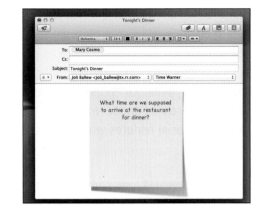

Attach a file or insert a picture

1. Click the Compose New Mail icon in Mail.

2. In the To window, type the email address of the intended email recipient. (If the contact is in your Address Book, it will fill in as you type.)

3. Type a subject in the subject line.

4. Type the message in the body of the email.

5. If you want to attach a file:

   a. Click the paperclip icon.

   b. Locate the file to attach and click Choose File.

   c. To select multiple files, hold down the Control key.

6. To add a picture:

   a. Click the Photo Browser icon.

   b. Locate the photo and drag it to the email.

   c. If applicable, resize the image by clicking an option from the bottom right corner of the email.

7. Complete the email and click Send.

As with other programs, email applications, etc., you can type text first and then format it, or you can select your formatting options beforehand. Unlike other email applications you may have used, you have access to various panes, including ones that let you easily drag and drop photos or apply stationery. Explore those features as time allows.

Important !

You won't be able to include pictures (among other things) in an email that also includes stationery if the stationery is limited in size.

Open attachments

If you receive an email with attachments, you'll see a paperclip icon in the message pane, as below. You can either click the icon for the attachment to open it in the message itself, or you can drag the attachment from the email body to the desktop. If you want to keep the attachment, you can drag it to the proper folder for long-term storage.

There are a number of other things you can do with Mail, but there's only so much space here. As time allows, click the various icons you see in Mail and in the New Message window and take a look at everything under each of Mail's menu bar options. You'll find you can show or hide CC and BCC lines in a new message window, choose which email address a message sends from by default, take 'quick looks' at attachments without opening them, check spelling and grammar, change the view, and more.

Minimise spam

Junk email (often referred to as spam) is email you don't want from people you do not know. Email that Mail thinks is junk is shown in gold in your Inbox. You may have seen items in gold in previous sections' screen shots. You'll want to train Mail so that it knows when an email is junk and when it isn't. You can start by locating any email listed in gold that isn't junk email and then clicking Not Junk from Mail's toolbar. The Not Junk icon looks like a thumbs-up. You'll see the thumbs-up icon only when you've selected an email that Mail has flagged as spam. By clicking this icon you're telling Mail that this is mail you would in fact like to receive.

Open and save an attachment

1 Select an email that contains an attachment.

2 Either:

a. Double-click the icon for the attachment to open it, and click File>Save or File>Save As.

Or

b. Drag the attachment icon to the desktop or to another area of your Mac to save it.

?

Did you know?

If you want to save an email so you can complete it later (because you aren't ready to send it yet), click the red circle in the New Message window and, when prompted, click Save. You can find the email later in Drafts, when you're ready to complete it.

Use Mail (cont.)

Minimise spam

1. Click any email that Mail thinks is junk.

2. If it is not junk, click Not Junk (thumbs-up).

3. Click any email that Mail thinks is not junk.

4. If it is junk, click Junk (thumbs-down).

5. To configure junk email preferences:

   a. Click Mail>Preferences from the menu bar.

   b. Click Junk Mail.

   c. Configure junk mail options as desired.

Alternatively, when an email arrives in your inbox that actually is junk email but it is not flagged, you should tell Mail that you don't know that person and that the email is indeed junk. You do this by selecting the email and clicking the thumbs-down icon – this is the Junk icon.

If you'd rather not manually teach Mail what's junk and what isn't, you can set the Junk mail preferences so that a specific thing happens when what Mail deems junk mail arrives. You access these options from the menu bar. Click Mail, click Preferences and click the Junk Mail tab. One option is to move all mail that is flagged as junk directly to the Junk mailbox. If you opt for this, make sure you check that folder a few times a week in case mail you actually want gets sent there.

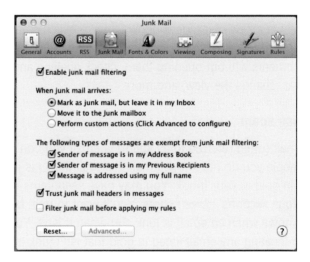

As you get to know Mail, you'll find that you can think of many ways that Mail could be personalised to better suit your needs. From the Preferences pane, you may find just what you're looking for to enhance or otherwise streamline the experience. To access Mail's preferences, click the Mail menu and select Preferences. Once there, explore these tabs:

■ From the General tab, you can choose how often to check for new emails and what alert to sound when they arrive. The Dock unread count option can be configured to show unread messages for the various mailboxes (Inbox Only or All Mailboxes, including Junk). Other options here include where downloaded attachments are stored and criteria for searching mailboxes.

■ Using Accounts preferences, you can edit your email account and add or delete extra accounts (there's no rule against having more than one email account). You can also direct the way your ISP's email servers respond to you collecting messages. Using the Advanced tab, choose which accounts to include when Mail checks for emails for you. You can also set when emails are removed from the mail server.

■ Use the RSS preferences to choose a default RSS reader, how often feeds are checked and what happens to them when they're received.

■ Junk Email lets you configure what happens when junk email arrives and which messages should be exempt from junk mail filtering.

■ Fonts & Colors lets you choose the font used for the message list, messages and notes, and apply other font options.

■ Viewing lets you change how Mail is laid out and what's shown when messages arrive. You can change how many lines appear in the list preview, for instance, and whether or not to display remote images in HTML messages.

■ The Composing tab lets you change the default email message format and configure how and when to check spelling. You can opt to include all the original message in your replies, too, and what account to use to send email by default.

Customise Mail (cont.)

Customise Mail by selecting a font for all new messages

1 Click Mail and click Preferences.

2 Click the Fonts & Colors tab.

3 Next to Message font, click Select.

4 Choose a font, font size and typeface.

5 Close the Fonts window.

6 Close the Preferences window.

■ The Signatures tab lets you easily create signatures for outgoing messages. You can opt to match the signature with the font you use when composing the message, among other things.

■ Use the Rules tab to create rules for mail. You can create rules for almost any scenario imaginable. Here I illustrate just a few of the ways you can start a rule.

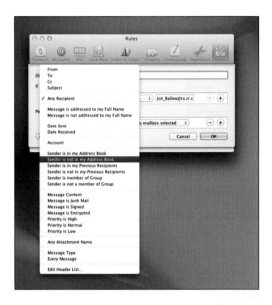

There are two more Lion-specific features I'd like to discuss before leaving Mail. One is to view your email by conversations, which combines emails in a single 'thread' into one. The other is to perform unique searches for mail you've misplaced.

When you opt to view your email in 'conversations', it allows you to view all your back-and-forth emails with a person (or a group of people) in one email window. When emails are grouped, you can easily locate all of them and view the progress of the conversation.

To enable this feature, click View>Organize by Conversation. Now click View>Expand All Conversation to understand how the grouping feature works. (Later you can collapse them in the same manner.) Grouped conversations appear in blue. Singular emails that are not part of any conversation remain white.

Lion's Mail offers powerful new search features. When you search for something, search suggestions help you find what you're looking for. Just start typing something in the Spotlight Search window and take a look at the matches. As you type, you'll see results, and you'll notice a few new things on the bar that runs across the top of Mail. For instance, you'll have the option to look only in a specific Inbox. Here's an example of some results. Emails matching those results will also appear and you can select any one of them in the list to open it.

Explore more Lion-only Mail features

6

For your information

You can learn much more about new Lion features for Mail at *www.apple.com*. Search for Lion and Mail.

Explore iCal

iCal is a program included with your Mac that offers a place to manage a calendar and events. iCal is available from the Dock, but you can find it from the Applications window in Finder too. Here, iCal is shown in Month view. You use iCal effectively by inputting information about upcoming events and creating reminders for them. An event can be an appointment, a date, a birthday or anniversary – it's up to you. When you create an event, you have the option to invite others to it as well and you can keep track of their responses easily.

You can create additional calendars to separate your appointments and events if you wear a lot of 'hats'. You may create a calendar for travel, sports and your children, for instance, and another for volunteer work or 'me time'. You can then view those calendars together or separately. Additionally, you can sync iCal with other calendars you keep, including those from Yahoo! or Google, and then sync it all to an iPhone or iPad, for example.

Your first step is to create a few events in iCal and create reminders for those events. Later, you can explore how you can create invitations and invite people to join you in the events you create. As you continue to use the applications, you'll discover you can subscribe to others' calendars as well, set preferences, and even change what day of the week your week starts. Here we'll only touch on what you can do; it'll be up to you to explore more on your own.

Did you know?

Many email programs can open iCal events you send, even Windows computers, but not all can. If compatible, recipients can accept or decline your invitation from their email program and you'll receive a response. You can then keep track of those responses using iCal and Mail.

If you've decided to create additional calendars in iCal, click the File menu and click New Calendar. If you've already told iCal you want to incorporate another calendar (perhaps a Gmail calendar), you'll have the option to add another Gmail calendar or add one just for your Mac. By default, there are calendars already configured named Work and Home on your Mac. Once you've configured the calendars you want and need, you can hide and show them by clicking Calendars in iCal. (Calendars is next to the + sign.) When a calendar in the list has a tick beside it, events on that calendar will appear in iCal in the colour configured to represent them.

Finally, from the iCal menu click Preferences. Use the tabs here to configure how many days a week your calendars should show, what day to start the week on, when the day starts and ends, and what the default calendar should be. By default, a birthday calendar will show, and birthdays will appear there for the contacts you keep if you input the information and iCal has access to it. You can also opt to turn off all alerts, delete events after a specific period of time, and more.

Create an event in iCal

1 Open iCal.

2 Click File and click new Event (alternatively, you can click the + sign). Note the other options under File, including New Reminder, New Calendar and Print.

3 Type a name for the event and hit Enter on the keyboard.

4 In the new event box that appears, click to enter and edit the information that's available, including the date and time.

5 Click None, next to alert.

6 Choose an alert option.

7 If applicable, enter or edit the information related to the alert.

8 To invite others, click Add Invitees. Again, enter the desired information.

9 If desired, attach a file, add a URL (web page address) or write a note.

10 Click Done.

Explore Address Book

Let's take a look now at the Address Book. As you may guess, the Address Book holds contact information for people you email or otherwise communicate with. The Address Book is located on the Dock by default, but if you've moved it you can find it in the Applications window from Finder. The Address Book, iCal and Mail all work together, and much of this unity is incorporated through the contacts you'll acquire and input here.

You may find when you first open Address Book that your contacts are already there. Perhaps they were automatically uploaded from the information stored with Gmail or another web-based email account, or perhaps you've already input a few manually. As noted in the information box here, you can also use the File>Import command to locate addresses you've previously exported from another computer or mail client. Whatever the case, you'll want to get your contacts' information input here so that you can access it when you need it.

Manually create a contact in Address Book

1. Open Address Book.

2. In the middle of the Address Book interface, click the + sign to create a contact card.

3. Click in the available boxes and entries and type the desired information. You can use the Tab key to move among entries.

4. When you've finished, click Done.

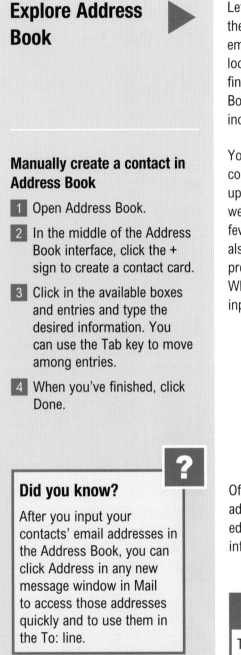

Often contact information changes, or you decide to add an address or a picture for a contact (among other things). To edit a contact, simply select it and click Edit to enter the new information.

Did you know?

After you input your contacts' email addresses in the Address Book, you can click Address in any new message window in Mail to access those addresses quickly and to use them in the To: line.

For your information

To import addresses stored on another computer, first use whatever means is necessary to 'export' those addresses. Save that contact information file somewhere you can access it from your Mac (perhaps a USB thumb drive). Then open Address Book and click File>Import. Follow the prompts to locate and import those email addresses so that they become contacts in Address Book.

Finally, if you have contacts configured in MobileMe, Yahoo! and Google, you can sync those contacts to your Mac. This provides a way to import contact information without entering it all manually. To do this, open Address Book and click Address Book>Preferences. Click the Accounts tab. Choose which online entity you'd like to sync with and click Configure. Type your email address and password, then click OK. You can then choose how you want to sync the contacts available. Generally Merge is best.

Edit a contact

1 Locate the contact to edit in Address Book. (You can search for it using the Spotlight Search window.)

2 Click Edit.

3 Click any entry in the card to edit it. Consider double-clicking the empty picture placeholder to add a picture.

4 Enter the desired information (or browse for a photo to use).

5 Click Done when you've finished.

?

Did you know?

With Address Book active, click Address Book>Preferences. You can opt to show the items in your Address Book in a different order (sort by last name, for instance), among other things.

Explore Address Book (cont.)

After you've set up Mail, explored iCal and added or imported your contacts, you'll start to see how all of these apps work together. For instance, in a new email message in Mail, you won't have to type a person's entire email address. As you begin typing their name, options will appear fom which you can select. Below is an example. I've only typed Cosmo, yet the entire email address appears, along with others (not shown) that also contain Cosmo in the address.

The same thing will happen when you use FaceTime. FaceTime is an application that lets you hold a video conversation with other contacts who also use FaceTime. In FaceTime, your contacts will be listed. Even iPhoto has an option to share images via email, and again you can simply start typing a name and matching addresses will appear automatically.

Networking and sharing

Introduction

It's highly unlikely that your Mac will always stand alone and that you'll never use it to join or participate in some kind of network. You might connect your laptop to a free Wi-Fi hotspot at the local coffee shop to access the Internet, or connect your desktop computer to your home network to share data, for instance. You might even connect to another Mac for a few minutes to exchange files through a private, temporary network you create.

Networking is an important feature and concept, enabling you to share resources with other network users and, once configured, you'll probably use it often. Some of the resources you can share on a network are printers, disk drives, music files, video files, pictures and business data, although there are others.

In addition to joining your Mac to a network and sharing data over it, you may decide to allow another person to use your Mac. Your Mac can support multiple users and this support enables those users to have a unique experience on the Mac each time they log on. This means you can create an account for your spouse, child or coworker, and they can use your Mac securely. These users will have access to their own desktop wallpaper, file folders, passwords, email accounts in Mail, and screen savers, among other things, every time they log on. You'll create user accounts for people you want to access your Mac over the network too, even if they don't plan to sit down at your machine and use it. User accounts help secure your Mac.

What you'll do

Connect two Macs with Ethernet

Use Lion's new AirDrop to connect two Macs wirelessly

Connect a Mac to a device with Bluetooth

Connect to a private Wi-Fi network

Connect to a public Wi-Fi network

Connect to a private network with Ethernet

Join a Windows workgroup

Connect to another computer on the network

Create a new user account

Enable file and folder sharing

Share a folder

Configure sharing options for a folder

Access a Mac's shared folders from a Windows computer

Share a printer

Connect to another device

Sometimes you'll want to connect to another Mac to exchange files, play a game or share media. If the Mac is not connected to your home network, or there's no network to connect to, you can create your own temporary network. You can connect two Macs with an Ethernet cable, and you can incorporate Lion's new AirDrop feature if you want to share between two new Macs wirelessly. There are other ways, too: you can set up various other kinds of ad-hoc networks, including wireless ones, though I won't discuss those here since AirDrop is so easy to use. You can also use your Mac to connect to devices that support Bluetooth and Bluetooth file transfers. That's a tad trickier, perhaps not to set up but to actually exchange files. However, I've included the basics here in case you want to give it a shot.

Connect two Macs with Ethernet

A simple way to link two Macs, perhaps a friend's older MacBook and your Mac mini, is to connect them via their Ethernet ports with a single Ethernet cable. Connecting two Macs in this way will enable you to swap data at a high speed, play a network game, and essentially do anything else that can be achieved by connecting to any network. Take note though, networking in this manner is on its way out; in fact, some computers don't even offer an Ethernet port any more. Thus, you may find AirDrop a much more effective way to connect (or the only way). You may also be forced to email files, use USB flash drives or come up with other creative ways to share data.

To get started, link the Macs with the Ethernet cable and start them. Launch System Preferences and select the Network pane. Click Ethernet from the list on the left and make sure Using DHCP is selected in the pop-up Configure menu. Click Apply. Repeat the procedure for the second Mac. Once you know you're connected, you can configure what to share.

Once connected, launch System Preferences and select the Sharing pane from Internet & Network (or Internet & Wireless, depending on the OS). Choose the services you want. Consider enabling file sharing, printer sharing and DVD or CD sharing. Repeat on the second Mac if you want sharing in both directions.

Important

!

New MacBook Air computers from Apple don't come with an Ethernet port. This may be a deal breaker if you travel a lot and the hotels at which you stay offer Ethernet only (and no Wi-Fi).

You'll have to make sure now that the other user can access your files. The process for allowing access differs a little from OS to OS. Refer to the Share folders, drives and printers section later in this chapter if you're using Lion to learn how to share on your end. If you're networking with an older Mac, you may have to consult Apple's online documentation if you need step-by-step instructions.

Use Lion's new AirDrop to connect two Macs wirelessly

If you want to share files with someone who is nearby and you're both running Lion on your Macs, you can share those files using a new feature called AirDrop. With AirDrop, there's no need to set up any kind of ad-hoc network, connect and configure a local Wi-Fi network, connect with Ethernet, email each other the files, or use some other option. There's also no need to enter System Preferences or do any kind of configuration. All you have to do is click the AirDrop icon in the Finder Sidebar and your Mac automatically discovers other AirDrop users within about 10 metres of you. Once you've done that on both Macs, you can share files simply by dragging them from your computer to the AirDrop icon for the other. The user then accepts the transfer (or rejects it). Once accepted, the file transfers directly to that person's Downloads folder and is fully encrypted for security.

Jargon buster

DHCP – a technology that automatically assigns the proper network address to your computer so it can join the network. Without this technology, you'd have to input the various entries manually.

Connect to another device (cont.)

Connect your Mac to a device via Bluetooth

1 Open System Preferences and click Bluetooth.

2 Verify that the Mac's Bluetooth features are enabled.

3 Perform whatever steps are required to enable Bluetooth on the second device.

4 On your Mac, continuing from Step 2, click the + sign.

5 Select the device and click Continue.

6 At the device, do what's necessary to 'pair' the device (connect it).

7 On the Mac, click Quit to close the dialogue box.

8 On your Mac, click Sharing Setup.

9 Verify that Enable Bluetooth Sharing is selected and configure what to share.

Connect with Bluetooth

Bluetooth is a technology for communicating wirelessly with devices such as computers, mobile phones, digital cameras, PDAs, printers and more. With a range of around 10 metres, Bluetooth poses no threat of interference and requires no licence or fee; you simply set up the devices to communicate and exchange data. Although individual devices have their own set-up routines, the procedures are broadly similar and OS X has a Bluetooth Setup Assistant to simplify the process.

Once connected, you'll have to discover some way to share data between your Mac and the device. How you'll do this differs depending on the device you've chosen. Even though some devices, like iPads, appear to pair and connect, there's no way to transfer files between them (without a third-party app, if one exists). However, in some instances there is a viable way to transfer files – you'll just have to refer to your documentation to find out how to do it.

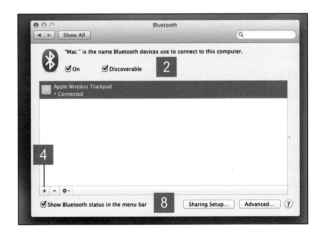

Important

If you have problems with your Mac maintaining a connection with a device, even after pairing is successful, on both devices opt to forget the devices. Then try again, this time initiating the pairing from the device, not from the Mac.

All Macs can connect to networks. If you have a desktop computer, you'll probably connect to your own home network or one where you work. If you have a laptop, the networks you connect to may include those at home or work, as well as free, open networks at coffee shops and libraries. Once you're connected to a network, if there are shared files and folders, or printers or other hardware available, you may have permission to access and use them.

You can also share the data you've saved to your Mac with others. There are two ways to do this. You can create a user account for another user and let that user log on to your Mac directly, or you can let a user access the folders you've shared over the network. Whatever you decide, you get to set who can access what by configuring the user accounts and shared folders you've created.

Connect to a private Wi-Fi network

One of the most common networking scenarios is a personal network that incorporates a networking device that allows for wireless connections. Often, this is a router, although it may be a switch or a hub. Routers are often connected to one other device, generally a cable, satellite or DSL modem, which allows access to the Internet.

Computers that are connected to the network via Wi-Fi can share their connected printers and other hardware, as well as music, video and other media. Of course data, such as word documents, presentations and databases, can be shared too. This kind of network is called a local area Wi-Fi network and is (or should be) protected with a password. You may have a local area network set up at your home, small business or workplace.

If you have a network at home or work, you can connect your Mac to it, provided it has the proper hardware. To connect to a Wi-Fi network, your Mac must support Wi-Fi connections. Almost all do. (If the network hardware allows you to connect via Ethernet only, your Mac will need an Ethernet port to connect. You'll learn how to do that later.) In the steps here, you'll learn how to connect to a secured, wireless network via Wi-Fi.

!

Important

It's important to note that in this book we're using Lion, the newest OS X version. Therefore, what's detailed here may not work exactly as described if you're using an earlier version.

Jargon buster

Router – a piece of hardware that is used to connect computers together to form a network, often for the purpose of sharing a single Internet connection, printers and data. Routers can transfer data between two unlike networks, too, such as the Internet and your home network.

Connect to a network (cont.)

Connect your Mac to a local, private Wi-Fi network

1 Turn on your Mac within range of a wireless network.

2 If you are prompted to join the network, click the prompt and type the required credentials.

3 If you are not prompted to join the network:

  a. Open System Preferences from the Dock or the Applications window.

  b. Click the lock and enter the proper credentials, if necessary, to unlock the settings options.

  c. Open Network and click Wi-Fi.

  d. Click Turn Wi-Fi On, if necessary. (In pre-Lion OSes, it's Turn AirPort On.)

  e. Under Network Name, select the network to join.

  f. Type in any required information, such as the password used to secure the wireless network.

4 Verify you're connected to the network in the left pane of the Network window.

Connect to a public Wi-Fi network

When you take your laptop to a public place such as a coffee shop, pub or hotel, you may find that the establishment offers a Wi-Fi network that enables you to connect to the Internet, for free. These types of networks are called 'hotspots' and are generally unsecured, meaning they do not require you to input a password. It's important to note that, while the network is 'free', some establishments *will* require you to buy a beer, get a library card or rent a room to gain access to the network. In a few instances, you may even be given a password, although everyone else on the network will be using that same password.

Because the network doesn't require a password to access it (or everyone in the vicinity knows it), two things are true: anyone can join and it's not secure. You should keep both of these things in mind while using the network. Be aware of your surroundings and when typing in passwords for websites, make sure no one is watching. Also, keep in mind that it *is* a

For your information

Your Mac should be less than 50 metres from the wireless router if you're indoors and less than 100 metres if outdoors.

public network. There may be people there 'snooping', hoping to pick up user names and passwords over the air. That said, it's best to use these kinds of networks to surf the Web and leave online shopping, accessing confidential data, etc. for a more secure network, like one in your home.

Connect to a private network with Ethernet

Ethernet is a common way to connect a computer to an existing network. You'll need an Ethernet cable to physically connect your Mac to the Ethernet-enabled hardware. This is called a 'wired' connection and the hardware you connect to is often a router. The problem with Ethernet, obviously, is the need to physically connect to a piece of hardware and stay connected to it. This limits mobility. However, many people prefer to connect via Ethernet when it is available (even if Wi-Fi is an option) because Ethernet is generally faster than Wi-Fi and can be more reliable. You may want to opt for Wi-Fi if you use a desktop computer and your connection to the network or the Internet is slower than you expect it to be. Ethernet cables come in all lengths, so you can probably find one that will reach from your Mac to the router in your office.

An Ethernet port on a computer looks very similar to a phone jack in a wall. It's square and the Ethernet cable pops into the port like a phone cord pops into a phone jack. Ethernet must continue to be an option on desktop computers because older networks, especially in small businesses where upgrading is expensive and difficult, offer only Ethernet as an option. With Ethernet, you also limit some network threats. For instance, hackers won't be able to pick up the data you send 'over the air', as they can in a Wi-Fi network.

!

Important

If you can't make changes to the existing settings, click the lock in the bottom left corner of the Network window. Input your administrator name and password as required.

Connect to a free Wi-Fi hotspot

7

1 Place your laptop within range of a free, unsecured Wi-Fi network.

2 When you see a prompt about joining that network, click it to join.

3 If you do not see a prompt:

a. Open System Preferences and click Network.

b. Click Wi-Fi (or AirPort on older Macs).

c. Enable Wi-Fi if necessary.

d. If Ask to join new networks is not enabled, enable it.

e. If prompted to apply the changes, click Apply.

f. When you see the prompt to join the network, select it.

Connect to a network (cont.)

Connect to a network with Ethernet

1. Open System Preferences, open Network and click Ethernet.

2. If you see Cable Unplugged, as shown here:

   a. Connect one end of an Ethernet cable to your Mac.

   b. Connect the other end of the cable to your router or other network hardware.

3. Leave Configure IPv4 set as Using DHCP.

4. Wait while the network is automatically configured.

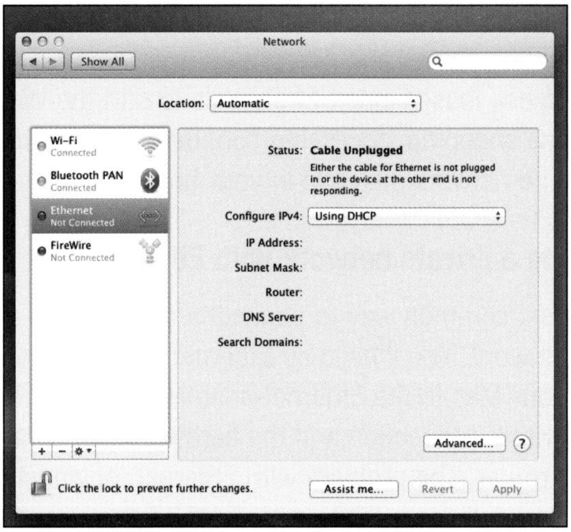

There are more Microsoft Windows computers in the world than there are Macs. Thus, it's safe to say that the majority of home networks are ruled by PCs and their networks were created using them. Those networks incorporate what's called a 'workgroup' to share files and folders, and the workgroup name can be anything the administrator desires. To really share files effectively, you'll have to connect to the network (which you've probably already done) *and* the workgroup (which you probably have not), and you'll have to configure sharing options. Although you'd think by now that sharing between Macs and Windows computers would be simple, alas it is not.

Alternatively, you may be a member of a Mac-only household, complete with an AirPort TV and other AirPort devices, and have a spouse who has purchased a Windows PC. This is less common, but certainly a viable scenario. Your spouse now wants to share files and folders with you and your Mac over the existing home network. In this case, you'll have to configure your Mac so that the Windows computer is welcome, and then teach your Windows user how to access your shared files. Again, something that should seem simple by now, but is not.

Join a Windows workgroup

You can join a network and gain access to the Internet, but if you want to join an existing Windows workgroup, you'll have to perform a few more steps. You won't be able to access shared data with the workgroup computers (certainly not easily) until you join.

Jargon buster

Workgroup – Windows term for a group of computers all belonging to the same network. Common workgroup names are MSHOME and WORKGROUP.

Working with Microsoft Windows

7

Did you know?

Even die-hard Mac users will find themselves in situations where they need to connect to a network that also incorporates Windows-based computers, or to share data with Windows PCs.

Working with Microsoft Windows (cont.)

Join a Windows workgroup

1 Open System Preferences and then Network. If applicable, click the lock to enable changes.

2 Choose the connection in the left pane that's active. It's probably Wi-Fi (AirPort) or Ethernet.

3 Click Advanced.

4 From the WINS tab, type a name for your Mac or keep the one that's assigned already.

5 Type the name of the Windows workgroup to join.

6 Click OK, and click Apply.

! Important

It may take a few minutes for you to see other compatible computers in the Finder. However, you may not see the Windows-based computers until you've 'mounted' them, detailed next.

Connect to a Windows computer on the network

After you've connected to the Windows network and joined the workgroup, you may have to *mount* the Windows computer so that you have access to it from your Mac. Unless you configure it so that the computer mounts automatically at login, you may also be required to manually connect to the networked computer each time you boot your Mac. Alternatively, you may be able to see computers without mounting them. What you see and have access to depends on how the shared computers are configured and shared. Whatever the case, you need to gain access to the shared computer(s) in the Finder, and sometimes this means mounting them. In this image there are two computers, one named nyc-cl20, the other named compaq. The former was manually mounted, the latter simply appeared.

Jargon buster

Mounting – makes a hard disk or disk partition accessible to a computer. Mounting a disk 'activates' it and makes the folders and files on the disk available to a user.

4 [points to Server Address: smb://NYC-CL20]

5 [points to + button]

6 [points to Connect button]

If, after connecting to a Windows computer (server), you decide you want to connect to that computer automatically (or a folder on it) every time you log on to your Mac, you'll need to configure it in System Preferences. In System Preferences, click Users & Groups (this used to be Accounts), click your user name in the left pane and click Login Items in the right. Click the + sign and browse to the computer and folder to open and click Add. Place a tick in the folder and close System Preferences. Here I'll connect to my Brilliant Mac folder each time I log on to my Mac.

Working with Microsoft Windows (cont.)

Mount a Windows-based network computer

1 Open the Finder. If you can't see the computer to access, continue here.

2 From the menu bar, click Go.

3 Click Connect to Server.

4 Keep smb:// and replace the rest with the name of the Windows computer you want connect to.

5 Click the + sign to add the server to your list of Favorite Servers.

6 Select the server in the list and click Connect.

7 Input an administrator name and password used on the Windows computer.

8 Select the folder to connect to and click OK.

9 An icon for the Windows computer will appear in the Finder. Click it to see the shared folders.

?

Did you know?

You can delete servers from the Favorite Servers list by clicking the server and clicking Remove.

Share folders, drives and printers

The main purpose for creating a network, joining workgroups, mounting computers, etc. is to share data. Perhaps you want to keep all your media on your strongest, most reliable machine and allow others access to it. This is a common reason for networking. Sharing media serves many purposes: it reduces the need to keep duplicate date on multiple machines, it creates a single place to back up all your media and it makes the media easier to manage with regard to who has access to what.

Beyond sharing data though, you may want to share a single printer, a recordable DVD drive, a backup device like an external hard drive, a scanner or other hardware. There's no reason to put a printer in every room that has a computer when you can simply share a single printer with everyone, nor is there any reason to purchase multiple backup devices if one will suffice. There is also no point in keeping the same 50 GB of media on every machine in the house when you can store it on one and allow access to it by the others.

The first step to sharing access to your Mac (either by letting someone log in locally or through a network), the media on it, the hardware attached to it and other items you want to make available is to create a user account for each person you'd like to give access to. While this may seem extreme, time-consuming and possibly unnecessary, trust me, it's the best way to go. It doesn't take as long as you'd think either. Once you create user accounts you get to say who accesses what, when and how. If set up correctly, sharing can be a joy, not a chore.

Create a new user account or enable the Guest account

User accounts are a good thing, and you're in control of them. User accounts let you log out and let someone else log in, if that's what you want. In doing so, OS X will create an entirely separate working environment for the new user, keeping your files and all your settings private as well as theirs. The other user(s) can customise the desktop, change preferences for the Dock, Dashboard and any other application, and generally set up the Mac the way they like it. However, when you next log in the Mac will be exactly as you left it.

It's important to remember that when different users access the same Mac, it is as though they are actually accessing entirely different machines. To swap data – a picture, say – you can't simply leave it on the desktop and expect the other user to be able to see it. Instead, you have to access a Public folder and put the picture in there. Additionally, you can't access any other users' data unless they specifically share the data with you. As you can see here, Jennifer's Public and Sites folders are available to all users, but Desktop, Documents, Downloads and the rest are not. If someone other than Jennifer tries to open these private folders, they are denied access.

If you don't want someone to sit down at your Mac and log on, you should still create user accounts for people you want to be able to access the data on your computer via your home network. This lets you control what they can access. For instance, you can allow your spouse to access folders named Taxes and Health that are stored on your Mac, but not access another personal folder you keep named Journal. And accounts aren't just for Mac users either. You can create a user account for a Windows user on your network and later share files with them over the network by making configuration changes in System Preferences>Sharing>File Sharing>Options (see overleaf).

Share folders, drives and printers (cont.)

Create a new user account

1 Open System Preferences.

2 Click Users & Groups (this is Accounts in pre-Lion OSes).

3 If necessary, click the lock so that you can make changes.

4 Click the + sign just above the lock icon.

5 Fill in the required information for the new user and click Create User.

! **Important**

If you create a user account for the person (or people) you want to share with before you actually share anything, you will avoid potential sharing problems later.

You won't always want or need to create a user account for every person who needs to use your Mac. For instance, if a friend wants to check their email or place a last-minute bid in an online auction, you'd hardly expect to have to create a user account for a few minutes of access. The same holds for an overnight guest like an aunt or uncle, or a neighbour who drops by for a quick favour (and to check their email). While you could simply let whoever needs quick access use your computer via your own account, remember, anyone who uses your account has complete control over all your files and settings. It's really not a good idea; it's just not secure.

Whether purposeful or not, a friend could harm your computer by opening an email that contains a virus, access your private and personal files, or download something harmful from the Internet. It's best to let all friends, neighbours or guests use the Guest account.

The nice thing about the Guest account, beyond its obvious security features, is that it's limited. A user can't do much and can't cause too much damage. Also, this separate account provides a clean desktop and *new-user* system settings for anyone who logs in using it.

To set up the Guest Account, launch System Preferences, select the Users & Groups option and click the Guest User account in the list on the left. Now tick the box Allow guests to log in to this computer.

Enable file and folder sharing

Once you're connected to your home network you can share data with others who are also part of that network. For instance, you may have a folder on your Mac that contains pictures from a recent holiday, and you want your spouse to be able to view those pictures from his own computer, through the network. You may want to configure similar sharing options for folders you've created, such as Travel or Funny Jokes. There are two steps to achieving this. The first is to enable File Sharing, the second is to choose which folder to share and configure Sharing Preferences.

?

Did you know?

In Users & Groups, you can click your user name to change your password or enable login items. You can select other accounts too, provided you're an administrator, and assign parental controls, among other things.

? 7

Did you know?

When a guest logs out, all information and files in the Guest account's home folder are deleted.

!

Important

Remember, if you can't make changes to the existing settings, click the lock in the bottom left corner and enter an administrator's name and password.

Share folders, drives and printers (cont.)

Did you know?

You can also enable Printer Sharing and DVD or CD Sharing here.

To enable File Sharing:

1. Open System Preferences.

2. Open Sharing.

3. Place a tick in File Sharing and click Options.

4. To share files with other Apple computers, tick Share files and folders using AFP.

5. To share files and folders with Windows computers, tick Share files and folders using SMB (Windows). Then:

   a. Place a tick by each user you want to allow access for.

   b. Input the password for the user account.

6. Click Done and leave the window open for the next section.

Once you've enabled sharing, you must then add folders to share and state how to share them.

Configure what to share and with whom

With File Sharing enabled you can now decide which folders you want to share. You can share default folders as well as any folders you've created yourself. Continuing from where you left off in the previous section:

1. Click the + sign under Shared Folders.

2. Locate and select the folder you want to share. Click Add.

3. Repeat these steps to add every folder you'd like to share.

Note how the folder is shared by default. In the next section, you'll learn how to configure those sharing options. (Leave this window open for now.) What is important to know right now is that sharing isn't an all-or-nothing configuration; you can choose which users can access which shares, and set exactly what those users can do once they have access.

Continuing from the previous section you will now configure who can access the folders you've shared and what they can do once they have acquired access.

1. Select any folder you've shared.

2. For any user listed, review the permissions granted. Note that the group 'Everyone' can read most folders. You might consider changing that to No Access.

3. To add a user who's not in the list:

   a. Click the + sign under Users.

   b. Verify Users & Groups is selected and select a user.

   c. Click Select.

4. To configure a user in the list:

   a. Click the arrow beside the user's name.

   b. Select a permission.

Important

It may take a few minutes for the newly shared folders to appear on the users' computers.

Access a Mac's shared folders from a Windows computer

▶

After you've shared folders with other users on your network, you may need to offer a tutorial for your Windows users so they know how to access those shared folders. Depending on the permissions applied to that folder for the user who has access, the user may be able to read what is in the folder or they may be able to make changes (write), too. Whatever the case, it's always best to test access anyway so that you're sure the user can access the folder when they wish.

Access a Mac's shared folder from a Windows PC

1 Open Windows Explorer.

2 Expand Network.

3 Expand the Mac computer.

4 Browse the shared folders.

You set up printer sharing the same way you set up file sharing. Open System Preferences, click Sharing and place a tick in the service box marked Printer Sharing in the left pane. Once printer sharing is enabled, you can configure how to share the printer, who to share it with and configure additional print options. One of the main items to configure is to limit who can print.

One way to do this is to remove people from the print list who you do not want to print, change the setting for Everyone to No Access, and then add specific people who are allowed to print. You can add people to this list by clicking the + sign shown here.

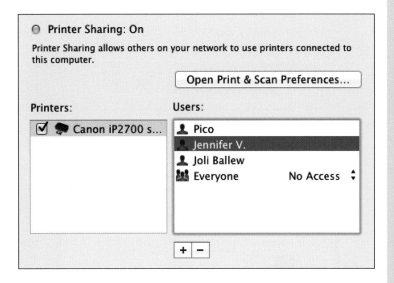

Share a printer (cont.)

Users will access the shared printer when they're ready to print to it. You can locate the printer from any application's Print dialogue box, even on a Windows computer as shown here. Accessing the shared printer is detailed here using Microsoft Word, but the same process will usually work for other programs.

1. Click the File button and click Print.

2. Choose the shared printer.

3. Configure settings as desired and then click OK.

4. Click Print.

Manage media with iTunes

8

Introduction

Media is a broad term that is used to represent just about anything you can view, read or listen to. On your computer this can be music, home videos, movies and audiobooks. It can also be pictures, radio shows, podcasts, TV shows, even playlists of your favourite songs.

You will acquire media from various sources, including your own music CD collection, which you can copy to your Mac, for free. You can also import media stored and shared on other computers on your network, you can purchase media from third-party sources such as Amazon and Audible, and you can purchase media from the iTunes Store. You can even transfer music purchases you've made to iPods, etc. to your Mac. In a nutshell, iTunes, included with all Apple OSes, is what you'll use to manage and listen to the media you acquire.

1

What you'll do

Check for iTunes updates

Explore the iTunes interface

Listen to a song or a CD

Copy CDs

Import media to the iTunes library

Share your iTunes library

Burn CDs

Create a smart playlist

Use the Mini Player

Explore the iTunes Store

Purchase media from the iTunes Store

Listen to the radio, podcasts and iTunes U

3

Explore the
iTunes interface

If you listen to a lot of music on your Mac, purchase movies from iTunes, listen to audiobooks or the radio, subscribe to podcasts or enjoy similar media, you'll probably use iTunes a lot. With iTunes, you can access the media stored on your Mac and import and access any shared media on your network. You can also use iTunes to sync with mobile devices you use, such as iPhones, iPads and iPods. Finally, you can use iTunes to enter the iTunes Store, where you can purchase media of all kinds, including media you've never explored, such as iTunes U lectures and museum tours.

The very first time you open iTunes, you should see the Welcome screen. If you don't, it's easy to find – just click Help from the menu bar and choose iTunes Tutorials. These video tutorials guide you through some of the most common tasks you'll do with iTunes, including importing music from the CDs you own and syncing your iTunes library with an iPod.

If you have some time to spend with the video tutorials, do so. Some of these are very informative and won't be covered in this chapter. When you've finished, simply click the red X in the top left corner of the tutorial window to close it. iTunes will remain open.

The next thing you should do is to check iTunes for updates. Apple offers updates regularly, and if you've never used iTunes or dismissed these updates as you were informed of them, you'll want to get them now before continuing. You'll be able to upgrade iTunes no matter what OS version you're using.

1. Open iTunes.
2. Click iTunes>Check for Updates. If updates are available, install them.

Once you're ready to use iTunes, you should familiarise yourself with the interface. Take a look at the left pane. It's separated into various sections, including Library, Store, Genius and Playlists.

- Library – this section offers access to your personal media. You'll find Music, Movies, TV Shows, Podcasts, iTunes U, Books, Apps, Radio and possibly others, depending on the media you've acquired. Click any library to view its contents in the middle pane. Here, Music is selected. Note the view that I've selected is Thumbnails. You can also view items in various types of lists and in Cover Flow view.

For your information

iTunes is available from the Dock by default, but it's also available from the Applications window in the Finder if you've moved it.

8

Did you know?

You will also see Devices in the left pane of iTunes if you have connected compatible devices to your Mac.

Explore the
iTunes interface
(cont.)

Play a song in iTunes

1. Open iTunes.

2. In the left pane, click Music. (Change the view if you wish.)

3. Browse through the music on your computer if there is any and locate a song to play.

4. Click or double-click the song to play it.

5. Explore the controls available to rewind, pause/play and fast forward.

■ Store – if you're connected to the Internet, click iTunes Store now. At the store, you can browse, purchase and download all types of media, from TV shows to apps to music and podcasts.

■ Genius – when Genius is enabled (Store>Turn On Genius; Store>Update Genius), the iTunes Store will suggest media you might like based on what you've already purchased or media you have on your computer. You can also create 'genius playlists' based on a single song you like, and iTunes will pick similar songs for the list.

■ Playlists – these are lists you create to group media you feel should be grouped together. You can create a playlist of your favourite songs and then copy those songs to a CD, for instance, or you can create a playlist that contains songs you like to exercise to or drive with. You can also access playlists that are already created for you, such as Recently Added and Recently Played.

While exploring the interface, make sure to note the playback controls, including rewind, pause/play, fast forward, the volume slider and the window that offers information about the song that's playing. As with other windows you'll have access to various view options and a Spotlight Search window. These options work the same in iTunes as in other windows – you simply need to click or search as usual to use them.

For your information

The right pane is the iTunes Sidebar, which offers information related to the selected media. You can enable and disable the Sidebar from the View menu, and there's a small icon in the bottom right corner of the iTunes window that toggles the Sidebar off and on.

Finally, as you explore iTunes you'll notice that when you connect a device such as an iPhone, iPod or iPad, a new item appears in the left pane. Also, you'll see a new entry when you insert a music CD. Go ahead and insert a music CD if you have one, or connect an i-device, as applicable. Here you can see two items under Devices: Joli's iPhone and a music CD called Mrs. Crowe's Blue Waltz. Note that both have eject buttons beside them.

```
STORE
    iTunes Store
    Ping
    Purchased

DEVICES
  ▶  Joli's iPhone              ⊏▪⊐  ⏏
       Mrs. Crowe's Blue Waltz        ⏏

GENIUS
    Genius

PLAYLISTS
```

For your information

When you insert a music CD into the CD drive on your Mac, iTunes will open and ask you if you want to import the songs that are on the CD into your iTunes library. Import is Mac-speak for copy. You may want to copy the CD, or you may simply want to listen to the songs on it.

Did you know?

When one song in the list ends, the next one will begin automatically.

Explore the iTunes interface (cont.)

Listen to a CD

1 Using the Finder, make sure there's no CD or DVD currently in the drive. If there is, click the eject button, an up-facing arrow.

2 Insert the music CD carefully, pushing slowly until the CD is accepted.

3 When prompted to import the CD, leave Do not ask me again deselected and click No.

4 Click the CD in the left pane of iTunes.

5 Double-click any song in the list to play it.

6 When you're ready to eject the CD:

   a. Click the eject button in iTunes, under Devices.

   Or

   b. On the desktop, drag the CD's icon to the Trash.

8

Build and share your iTunes library ▶

You may not have much media on your Mac. However, you may have media on other computers, in a CD collection, on an i-device, on an MP3 player or in other places like a music folder on a networked computer. You can transfer that media to your Mac in various ways. One of the easiest ways to get music on to your Mac is to rip your CD collection, so that's where you'll start.

Rip a CD

1 Slowly insert a CD you'd like to copy.

2 If you see the prompt shown here, click Yes.

3 Deselect any songs you don't want to copy.

4 Note you can access Import Settings or Stop Importing from the iTunes window.

Rip CDs and copy already ripped music

You can copy songs from CDs you own to your Mac. This is known as 'ripping a CD', even though you aren't technically 'ripping off' anything. You may opt to rip your entire CD collection so that you can listen to music without inserting CDs, to create your own CDs that contain mixes of your favourite songs, to share the music with networked computers or to copy those songs to other devices you own, such as iPads or iPhones. Ripping a CD collection is the first place to start when populating iTunes (and your Mac) with music.

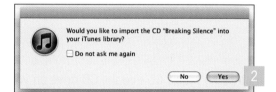

For your information ⓘ

Ripped songs will be stored in a file format called AAC. If you want to sync the ripped songs to a generic MP3 player like a Sony Walkman, you'll want to change the Import Settings so that songs are ripped using the MP3 Encoder format instead. You can make the change in iTunes>Preferences, from the General tab, under Import Settings.

Important ❗

For now, don't select Do not ask me again at any prompt.

If you've already ripped your collection to another computer on your home network, don't rip the songs all again. Instead, copy what you've already ripped over the network. One way to do this is to 'import' those songs into your iTunes library, as detailed in the next section. If that doesn't work, return here and consider these other options:

■ Use AirPlay to transfer files between two non-networked Macs that run Lion.

■ Copy the media to a large USB drive and then copy the media on the drive to your Mac.

■ Position two Finder windows as shown below and drag and drop the files to copy between them. (You'll have to Control + click the Finder icon to open a second Finder window.)

Add shared media to your iTunes library

If your Mac is part of a network and you have access to the media on other networked computers, you can tell your Mac where to look for that media and to import it. As you explore this option, you may be surprised at all the media available to import. For that reason, it's best to import small pieces at a time (such as your iTunes folder) rather than, say, importing all the media in your Users folder right at the start. It's also important to understand what you're importing. Your Mac will import multiple copies of the same songs, which can pile up and frustrate you if you have too many duplicates to sift through.

?

Did you know?

During the import process, a green tick means the song imported successfully, a red X means it did not, and an orange squiggly line means it's currently importing.

8

!

Important

As you can see in this image, I'm transferring quite a few duplicate songs. No matter what route you take to copy your media files, you should try to avoid copying duplicate data, to make your media easier to manage.

Build and share your iTunes library (cont.)

Import media to the iTunes Library

1. In iTunes, click File>Add to Library.

2. Browse to the location of the shared media. Note you may have to mount a server from the Go menu to have access to it from the Finder.

3. Select the folder, perhaps Music or a subfolder in it, and click Choose.

4. Wait while the media imports.

5. If you see new libraries in the left pane of iTunes, click to see the newly imported media.

6. Repeat to import other media folders as desired.

There are additional ways to get media on your Mac, although I won't cover them all here. Most involve connecting a device and then dragging and dropping the desired media to the proper folder on your Mac. (You can copy movies to the Movies folder, for instance, and music to the Music folder.) However, one last notable way is to connect an iPad, iPod or iPhone, select it from the left pane of iTunes and from the File menu select Transfer Purchases.

For your information

You can import music, audiobooks, movies and more, provided you have the proper rights, permissions and user names and passwords. You'll be prompted if a password is necessary.

Share your iTunes media

Now that you have a bunch of media on your Mac, you can share it with others on your network. Sharing helps keep duplicates from being created across computers and lets you listen to the media on your Mac in other areas of the house.

You have to manually set up media sharing:

1. From the menu bar, click iTunes.

2. Click Preferences.

3. From the Preferences window, click the Sharing tab.

4. Tick Share my library on my local network.

5. Configure what to share, whether a password is required and other options.

6. Click OK.

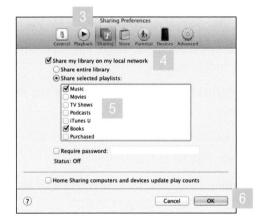

Did you know?

You can protect children from accessing content that is not appropriate for them by either requiring a password or sharing specific playlists only.

8

Did you know?

Some of the playlists you see in iTunes are updated regularly to reflect your personal preferences. Top 25 Most Played is one of them. If you don't want others who access your media on the network to count towards your play counts, disable the option to let those users update play counts.

Burn a CD

Now that you have music on your Mac, you can go a step further and burn CDs that contain your favourite songs. You can listen to these in your car or on a compatible CD player. This is called 'burning a CD' because a laser actually burns the CD to write to it. It's legal to burn a CD for your personal use, although there's a law against burning, say, a bunch of copies of your favourite music mix and selling them to your friends! You burn a CD by adding songs to a playlist first, then choosing to copy (burn) that playlist to a CD.

To burn a CD:

1. If there's a CD in the CD drive, eject it.

2. Insert a blank, writeable CD.

3. If prompted, choose Open iTunes from the Action options and click OK.

4. Click File>New Playlist.

5. Type a name for the playlist and press Enter on the keyboard. (My playlist is entitled Songs for the Car.)

6. Click Music in the left pane, locate your favourite songs and drag them to this playlist.

7. With the playlist filled with songs you like and selected in the left pane:

   a. Control + Click the playlist.

   b. Click Burn Playlist to Disc.

8. Review settings and click Burn. The default disk format, Audio CD, is fine for CD players in cars.

	✔	Name	Time	Artist
1	✔	Jar of Hearts	4:07	Christina Perri
2	✔	Bad Day	3:54	Daniel Powter
3	✔	Saving Grace (Theme)	3:08	Everlast
4	✔	Welcome Me	4:36	Indigo Girls
5	✔	Jonas & Ezekial	4:08	Indigo Girls
6	✔	Ride Me Like A Wave	3:40	Janis Ian
7	✔	Tattoo	4:20	Janis Ian

Classical Music	
Music Videos	
My Top Rated	Open in New Window
Recently Added	
Recently Played	Export...
Top 25 Most Played	Burn Playlist to Disc
Driving Songs	
Genesis	Duplicate
	Delete
Songs for the Car	

You learned how to create a playlist in the previous section detailing how to burn a CD. Playlists are easy to create: just click File>New Playlist, name it and then drag the desired songs to it. With iTunes, you always create a playlist first and burn that playlist to a CD second. You can create playlists in a similar manner even if you don't want to burn that list to a CD. For instance, you might create a playlist that contains songs that motivate you to run faster or bike harder during your daily workout, then copy that list to your iPod and play it at the gym. You might create a playlist that contains the perfect music for a romantic dinner date and play that through your iPad when you have a dinner guest. Likewise, you might create a playlist that contains only music that makes you sleepy, perhaps one that contains the audio for a book on meditation, and play that when you go to bed, listening to it on your iPhone. Of course, you can listen to any playlist on your Mac, using iTunes.

Beyond these kinds of playlists are smart playlists. These are playlists that iTunes helps you create. You tell iTunes what criteria must be met and it helps you find songs that match them. Smart playlists change as the criteria you set are met. For instance, you might create a smart playlist that contains songs you've listened to 25 times or more. As you listen to more and more music, iTunes keeps track of what you listen to the most. Once a song meets any criteria you've set, it's added to the smart playlist you created. There are lots of types of criteria to set.

Think about the smart playlists you'd like to create. Consider these:

- A playlist that contains songs by a specific artist, selected at random by iTunes.

- A playlist that contains songs that are faster than a specific number of beats per minute that you set, to create a perfect workout partner.

- A playlist based on the date the songs were added to iTunes. You can configure any date and choose how many songs to include in the playlist.

- A playlist based on the date a song was released. Create playlists for your favourite years, such as 1982 or 1998.

Create a smart playlist

8

Create a smart playlist (cont.)

Create a smart playlist

1. With iTunes active, click File>New Smart Playlist.

2. Verify that Match the following rule is selected and configure criteria as desired.

3. Configure other options as desired, limiting the song list to a certain length or disallowing live updating.

4. Click OK.

5. Type a descriptive name for the playlist.

For your information

Select the playlist in the left pane to access it and play the songs in it.

As with other applications, iTunes in Lion can be viewed in full-screen mode. The keyboard shortcut is the up arrow + Command (or Windows) + F. However, most of the time what you're looking for with iTunes is the option to minimise it on the screen so you can work on other things while you listen to music, while at the same time maintaining access to the playback controls. This is where the Mini Player comes in handy. The Mini Player makes iTunes smaller, but offers controls so it's still functional.

When you're just learning about Mini Player mode, it's best to use the View menu; choose Switch to Mini Player. You can try the keyboard combinations you'll see there as you gain experience. Once in Mini Player mode, you can click the green circle in the top left corner to restore iTunes.

8

Explore the iTunes Store

The iTunes Store is a one-stop shop for all kinds of media. You can purchase music, movies, TV shows and similar media, and obtain free media including podcasts and college lectures from universities all over the world. The iTunes Store is separated into media categories to help you quickly navigate to the type of media you're interested in obtaining. There are quick links down the right side, and a Spotlight Search window to help you navigate to a specific media title or artist.

To more easily navigate the iTunes Store, familiarise yourself with the nine buttons that run across the top of the iTunes Store interface:

■ Home – click the Home icon any time you feel lost in the store or want to return to the Home page for iTunes.

■ Music – click the Music tab to go to the music part of the store. You'll find music you can purchase and music that's free. You'll also have quick access to the most popular songs and albums.

■ Movies – click the Movies tab to go to the Movies part of the store. You can download free movies, preorder movies that are soon to be released, browse movies by genre, even rent some movie titles.

■ TV Shows – click this tab to view TV entries. You can purchase entire seasons of shows or single shows. Those shows then belong to you and you can watch them as often as you like.

■ App Store – click the App Store tab to enter the store, where you can purchase apps for your Mac. You learned a little about the App Store earlier in this book.

■ Books – click the Books tab to explore e-books available for purchase. You'll need the iBooks app and an iPhone, iPad or iPod Touch to read them.

■ Podcasts – click this tab to browse podcasts that are available from the iTunes Store. You will find free items here, and you can browse both audio and video podcasts, among other things.

■ iTunes U – click the iTunes U tab to browse through college lectures from universities, browse K-12 offerings, and even watch videos taken in museums and other places of interest. You may even find free audiobooks here, although the quality won't be nearly as good as what you'd find at, say, *www.audible.com*.

■ Ping – click the Ping tab to find people to follow by searching for a name, by inviting friends, or by choosing people whom Ping recommends. Ping is a social networking feature, where you can create a profile and others can follow you to see what you're listening to, watching or reading.

8

Purchase media from the iTunes Store

It's easy to purchase (or obtain free) media from iTunes. You'll see the price in a button beside the media you've selected (or you'll see *Free*). You only need to click the price or the free button to start the purchasing process. You'll be prompted to input your password and to verify that you want to make the purchase, but it doesn't take more than a few seconds to get what you want.

Purchase media from the iTunes Store

1 Locate the media to purchase.

2 Click the price button beside it.

3 Tap Buy Song, Buy Album, or other prompt.

4 Input your password if required. This won't be necessary if you've recently made a purchase.

5 Click Buy.

6 Wait while the media downloads; you can watch it in the iTunes window at the top of the iTunes interface.

7 In the left pane of iTunes, click Purchased.

8 Click the item to play it.

Did you know?

If you purchase a movie, obtain a podcast, buy a TV show episode or download an app, look in their respective folders in the left pane – you'll see them there.

You may be wondering what some of the other offerings in iTunes actually relate to. You may be wondering how your Mac brings in radio stations, for instance, and if those are local or from places further away. (There's no antenna on your Mac that you know of, so local stations seem unlikely.) You may not know what a podcast is either, why podcasts are free, or what's available at iTunes U. Well, it's just media, like everything else in iTunes. It's just a different kind of media than you're used to.

Radio

Radio is a type of media. You access radio stations from the left pane of iTunes. Click Radio in that pane to get started. You'll immediately notice that indeed there is no 'local' category, and your Mac does not start broadcasting any radio station in the vicinity. Instead, you're offered a list of 'streams'. These streams come through the Internet and are separated into categories/genres. Click any down arrow to access the list of radio stations in any category.

All you have to do from here is click any radio station title to start listening to it. While you're listening, you can change the volume from inside the iTunes window (look to the right of the Stop button), from the menu bar, from external speakers and often from media-compatible keyboards.

8

Did you know?

The radio stations you listen to in iTunes come to you via the Internet. This is referred to as Internet radio.

Listen to the radio, podcasts and iTunes U (cont.)

Download and listen to a single podcast

1 In iTunes, in the left pane, click iTunes Store.

2 Across the top of the iTunes window, click Podcasts.

3 Browse the podcasts as you'd browse a web page, clicking links and using the Back button.

4 If you see a subscribe button only, click the name of the provider to access the podcast description page.

5 If you find a podcast you like and want to download:

a. Click Free beside the podcast to download.

b. Wait while the podcast downloads.

6 To listen to the podcast, click Podcasts in the left pane of iTunes.

7 Locate the podcast and click the Play icon.

Podcasts

A podcast is often an informative lecture, news show, sermon or educational series offered free from colleges, news stations, churches and similar entities. You can browse for free podcasts in the iTunes Store. If you find something you like, you can download a single podcast or subscribe to one to receive it on a schedule.

As you browse the list of podcasts and their providers, you'll probably recognise a few. You'll find podcasts from your local news stations, from sports stations, by comedians, musicians and other entertainers to promote themselves, and sometimes even by companies touting a new product.

If you find a podcast you like, you should start by downloading and listening to a single episode. If you like it and think you'll listen to this particular podcast regularly, consider subscribing to it. When you subscribe to a podcast, new podcasts will be downloaded automatically as they become available.

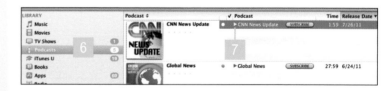

Important

When you subscribe to a podcast, it's downloaded automatically when a new podcast is available.

iTunes U

iTunes U, short for iTunes University, offers audio and video lectures and media from colleges and universities all over the world. The media available is free and can help you learn a new language or a new skill, learn about a topic such as quantum mechanics or business ethics, and even learn to do things such as take better pictures or mix music sound tracks.

In addition to lectures, you can browse museums virtually, listen to and watch experts describe museum artifacts, and explore information stored in the Library of Congress, among other places. You obtain iTunes U media the same way you obtain podcasts; you simply navigate to what you want to access and click it to download it to your Mac.

There are a few notable categories in iTunes:

■ Universities and Colleges – click here to locate a college or university by name and to narrow what's available by country. Click the individual college name to see what's available from that college.

■ Beyond Campus – click here to access educational offerings from off-campus institutions such as museums and opera houses.

Important

Before you leave this chapter, make sure you have some way to back up the media in your iTunes library. This is especially important if you've purchased an expensive movie, music albums or similar media. Consider setting up Time Machine for this task. You'll find this in System Preferences>Time Machine. There are other ways to back up your data, though, including dragging and dropping to an external drive, storing data on a networked computer, and even backing up music, apps and similar media to an iPad, for instance.

Photos, videos and webcams

Introduction

It's highly likely that you have some sort of device you can use to take pictures and videos. It may be a mobile phone, a smart phone, a digital camera or a digital video camera. You probably have some way to get those photos and videos on to your computer, too, perhaps by connecting the device to your Mac with a cable, sharing via Bluetooth, copying from a camera card, or even emailing the media on it to yourself. You may also have friends and family members who send you pictures and videos in emails, or you may have access to shared photos and videos on social networking websites like Facebook or Flickr. You may even record yourself with a webcam! While it's generally easy enough to take, record and view this kind of media, it's often much more difficult to manage it.

In this chapter you'll learn how iPhoto can help you manage all the pictures and videos you amass. You'll learn about how iPhoto can separate your photos into 'events' and how your Mac can be configured so that it recognises the people in your photos and groups the photos together. You'll learn how to edit photos, too, and even how to shorten a video.

After you've become familiar with iPhoto, you'll explore one more photo/video feature: communicating with audio and video through a webcam over the Internet. There are two ways to do this: you can communicate with video and text with iChat, or you can use Apple's newest offering for video calling, FaceTime.

What you'll do

Import photos

Explore the iPhoto interface

Tag people with Faces

Configure iPhoto preferences

Crop, straighten and fix red-eye in photos

Create a photo album

Create a slide show and add effects

Email a photo

Print a photo or order prints

View videos

Shorten a video

Use iChat

Use FaceTime

Open and populate iPhoto with pictures

▶

iPhoto looks like other apps and windows you've explored on your Mac. It resembles the Finder because it has similar sections in the left pane (Library and Recent). It resembles iTunes somewhat because it offers options for navigating and grouping the media however you like. Finally, it appears in a window, and there's a related menu bar that offers options you're already familiar with, such as File>Preferences. So relax, this is going to be a breeze!

You can open iPhoto from the Dock. (If it's not there, check the Applications folder.) The first time you open iPhoto, you'll be prompted about what you'd like iPhoto to do when you connect a digital camera. If you'd like to use iPhoto to assist you in uploading (copying) the photos on your camera to your Mac, click Yes. If you have other software you prefer, click No. If you aren't sure, click Decide Later.

Once you've made that choice, the iPhoto window will become visible. If you've never used iPhoto before, you may not see any photos. You'll need to tell iPhoto which photos you want it to manage for you and offer up for viewing. You can do this in several ways, all of which have to do with importing photos you like.

!

Important

Before you start importing every photo on every computer and on every camera you own, think about what you really want out of iPhoto. You don't want it to be cluttered with pictures you don't like, duplicates, or bad shots of boring subjects. So be careful and put some thought into it – only import pictures you enjoy and want to work with. You can always import more if you decide to later.

If you already have pictures on your Mac, think about which you like best and which you'd like to view and organise with iPhoto. You can then group those photos together in a folder and tell iPhoto to import it. You should do this to make sure you only import photos here that you actually like rather than simply every picture you own. I can tell you from experience that you're not going to want to wade through photos you don't like or never view; they'll just be in the way! Once you have the pictures grouped together that you'd like to import to iPhoto, you are ready to continue. (Note that if you *want* to import every picture you own, don't worry about this step.)

◀ **Import photos already on your Mac**

! Important

If you have videos on your computer, on a digital camera, on a networked computer or in other places, and those videos are stored in folders that also contain pictures, the videos will be imported with the pictures when you apply import commands. You can distinguish pictures from videos in iPhoto easily – videos have a 'play' arrow on them.

Once you're ready, you'll use the Import command to import photos into the iPhoto application. You can access the required command from the menu bar by clicking File>Import to Library. Then simply navigate to the folder containing the pictures and click Import.

9

Import photos already on your Mac (cont.)

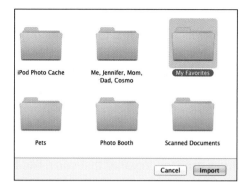

Import photos (and videos) already on your computer to iPhoto

1 Open iPhoto from the Dock or the Applications window.

2 When prompted whether to open iPhoto when you connect your digital camera, make any choice.

3 To import photos into iPhoto:

a. Click File>Import to Library.

b. Browse to any picture folder to add.

c. Click Import.

d. Repeat as desired.

For your information

iPhoto offers options, once photos are imported, to create photo projects such as photo books and invitations, to sync your picture library with Facebook, and to sort your pictures by faces, events, albums and more.

If you have a digital camera, you can copy the pictures on it to your Mac. If you don't have many pictures on your Mac yet, this is a great way to add some. When you plug in your camera, if you've configured iPhoto to import photos from it you'll see the icon for the device under Devices in iPhoto, and the pictures on it will be displayed in the main window. From there, you can name the event if there is one, select the photos to import and choose Import Selected. You can also opt to Import All.

You'll also see a new entry under Devices in iPhoto if you connect or insert something your Mac recognises as having photos on it. For instance, if you insert an SD card you've removed from your camera, you'll see it there. You may also see USB sticks, among other things. As you can see here, some devices may not have a name attached to them. This is a generic SD card, for instance.

Although it won't be automatic, you can pull pictures from a phone that can be connected and recognised by iPhoto, from external hard drives you may have used to back up photos from another computer, and from CDs and DVDs. As with other options, if you don't see the device in the iPhoto window, simply click File>Import to Library and browse to the pictures on the device.

Import photos (and videos) from a camera or similar device

Import pictures (and videos) from a digital camera

1 Connect the camera using its USB cable or remove the camera card and insert it into your Mac's card reader.

2 In iPhoto, select the item under Devices.

3 Hold down the Command key (or the Windows key on a Windows keyboard) to select individual pictures to import, if you wish.

4 Click Import Selected or Import All.

5 Choose what to do with the imported photos on your camera or card: Delete Photos or Keep Photos.

6 Note the new pictures under Recent>Last Import.

Did you know?

If you don't see the camera under Devices in iPhoto after connecting your camera, click File>Import to Library.

9

Copy pictures and videos from a networked computer

▶

If you've set up a network and have pictures stored on network computers (that you have access to), you can copy pictures from shared folders on those networked computers and put them on your Mac. You can either copy those photos to your Pictures folder or you can import the pictures directly to iPhoto. If you want to import directly into iPhoto, simply use File>Import to Library as detailed earlier. If you want to copy, you can use any technique. I prefer positioning two Finder windows side by side and dragging folders over, but there are many other options.

It's important to understand that if you've already imported, say, all of the photos in the Pictures folder, and you add photos to that folder now, those pictures will be imported into iPhoto automatically. That's because you've already told iPhoto to watch that folder and show you the pictures in it. It's probably best, then, if you want to keep iPhoto neat and tidy, to copy pictures from networked computers on to your Mac into a folder that's not already been selected to be imported to iPhoto. You could create a new folder in Finder called Network Photos, for instance, copy photos there and then import manually only what you want to see in iPhoto.

?

Did you know?

Hold down the Shift key to select multiple, contiguous pictures. Just click the first in the list and then the last and all the pictures in between will also be selected.

You may have pictures in a shoe box, in a photo album, in a plastic bin in the attic or in other places. The only way you're ever going to get those files on your Mac is to scan them (or have someone else scan them for you and put them on a DVD you can copy to your Mac). You should put this on your To-Do list if this is the case. Those photos are getting older and most likely deteriorating, and your family would probably enjoy looking at them digitally. (Also, once scanned, you can put them on Facebook!) If you have a scanner and pictures to scan, you have several options for doing so. It'll be up to you to decide which option is best for you. You'll need some sort of software and you have various options.

Important

Your scanner has to be Mac-compatible, installed, connected and turned on to function. If you are having problems with your scanner, check these things first.

◀ **Explore options for scanning pictures**

Explore options for scanning photos

- Press the button on the scanner and use the scanner software that appears.

- Open Preview, an app that comes with your Mac, and choose File>Import from Scanner.

- Use a third-party program like Photoshop Elements that includes commands such as 'Import from Scanner'.

- Use the Mac's Image Capture program. It's in the Applications folder. You can also use this program to import images from other devices, including SD cards and other compatible devices.

- Access and use a networked scanner.

9

Explore the
iPhoto interface

Now that you have some pictures in iPhoto, you can more easily and effectively explore the iPhoto application. As you've seen, there are various libraries in the left pane, as well as a category named Recent with Last Import, Last 12 Months and others. The best way to understand what each offers is to click each one.

Start with Events. Review the titles listed. Because you're already familiar with your own pictures, picture folders and even specific events, this will mean more to you than to anyone else. You'll be able to see how the Events folder is classified, organised and created easily.

While in the Events view, move your mouse from left to right (and back again) over each Events folder. You will see the pictures change. This allows you to easily view thumbnails of what's in the folder. If you like, when you see your favourite picture appear, use Command + click to access the contextual menu. Choose Make Key Photo from the options. The picture you set will be the 'cover' for that folder.

Click Photos in the left pane to see all your photos. You can scroll through the photos available using a scroll mouse or trackpad, or by dragging from the scroll bars on the right side of the iPhoto interface. This may be a good time to try out full-screen mode, too. Click the two arrows in the top right corner to invoke it (click Esc to restore the old view). Here is a picture I recently imported to the event I named *A tour of Brookhaven College*.

Explore the iPhoto interface (cont.)

Click Faces, then proceed as instructed to help your Mac figure out who is featured in your pictures. You can type a name for each person shown. You can continue to name people by clicking Show More Faces – depending on the size of your pictures library, you could be at it a while! When you're tired of verifying faces, click Continue to Faces. You'll be quite happy with the result.

Finally, click Places. Your photos will have places applied to them only if your Mac can somehow decipher where they were taken. Most phones embed location information, as can iPads, digital cameras and other devices. Pictures that have this embedded information (called metadata) can be classified by iPhoto and denoted with a pin in the location associated with it. If you see a pin, click it. Then click the location to see the related photos. Click Map when you've finished.

For your information

To increase or decrease the size of the thumbnails in, say, Events, Photos or Faces view, use the zoom slider at the bottom of the iPhoto window.

9

Explore the Places library

1 In iPhoto, click Places.

2 Click any pin.

3 Click the arrow that appears beside the location listed.

4 Browse the photos that appear.

5 To show the photo in its related event folder, Control + click and click Show Event.

6 Click Places again to return to the previous places view.

Explore the iPhoto interface (cont.)

Configure iPhoto preferences

1 Click iPhoto on the menu bar and click Preferences.

2 Click each tab once and configure choices as desired.

3 Close the Preferences pane when you've finished.

In order to make sure that iPhoto meets your needs, as with other apps, you should configure its preferences. There are five tabs available in the Preferences pane:

■ General – here you can configure a bit of what's shown under Recent, you can opt to show item counts, and change what you want iPhoto to do when you connect a camera. You can also opt to autosplit events by day, week and in other ways. Leave Check for iPhoto updates automatically enabled.

■ Appearance – here you can apply photo borders and backgrounds, and configure other appearance options.

■ Sharing – this tab enables you to share your photos with others on your network or those who have access to your computer. You can also require a password if you like. Alternatively, you can tell iPhoto you want it to look for and find photos others have shared.

■ Accounts – you can configure the email accounts you want to use with iPhoto here. This will be populated automatically with information in Mail, but you can remove accounts as desired. You may want to add the email address here that you use to upload pictures to a photo-sharing website, if applicable, or settings for a social networking site like Flickr. You may also want to remove certain accounts that you don't use very often and don't want people replying to.

■ Advanced – use the Advanced options to configure the program to use to edit photos (iPhoto is the default), if you want iPhoto to look up information for Places, and if you want to be blind CC'd on emails you send from iPhoto, among other things.

The Edit button is located at the bottom of the iPhoto window. When you click it, the editing options appear and include rotating the picture, enhancing it, fixing red-eye, straightening it, cropping it and retouching it. This makes editing pictures easy; everything you need to perform basic editing tasks is easily available. iPhoto can automatically enhance photos, too – you only need click the photo, click Edit and click Enhance.

Cropping

Almost every commercial image that you see reproduced in a newspaper or magazine has been cropped before publication. This means it's been trimmed so that anything not relevant to the picture is no longer part of it. Careful cropping can turn an otherwise ordinary picture into a truly eye-grabbing image. iPhoto offers an easy-to-use cropping tool you can use for the same purpose.

Cropping is simple. First locate the image to crop, click the Edit button and click Crop. To maintain a particular size or shape regardless of what you do with the cropping tool, tick Constrain and choose a size or shape from the pop-up menu. If desired, click and drag an edge or corner to resize the cropping box. Click anywhere within the area covered by the box to move it around the picture and home in on the section

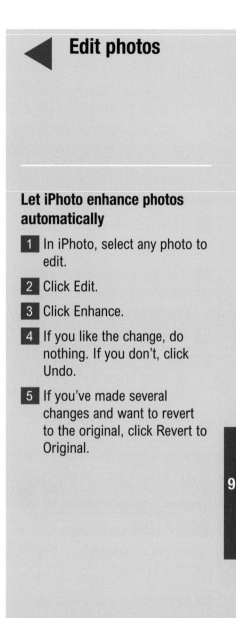

Let iPhoto enhance photos automatically

1. In iPhoto, select any photo to edit.

2. Click Edit.

3. Click Enhance.

4. If you like the change, do nothing. If you don't, click Undo.

5. If you've made several changes and want to revert to the original, click Revert to Original.

9

Edit photos (cont.)

Get rid of red-eye

1 Select a photo to fix.

2 Click Edit.

3 If necessary, use the zoom slider so you have access to the red eye in the image.

4 Click Fix Red-Eye.

5 Move the Size slider so that the circle is about the same size as the eye in the picture.

6 Click each eye to fix with the newly sized circle.

7 Click Done.

For your information

There are other editing options to explore. Try Retouch and Rotate. Retouch lets you click or drag over a blemish to remove it. Sometimes you can use this tool to remove scratches in an old photo you've scanned, discolorations on a subject's face, or even dirt on the clothing of a subject in a photo. Rotate lets you, well, rotate an image.

of the image you want. As you do so, a useful grid is displayed to help you define the areas of interest in the picture using the rule of thirds. When you've finished, just click Done.

Straightening

Unless you're claiming artistic licence, a picture that's crooked is really just a picture that would probably look better if it aligned with the horizontal or vertical. A shot of Pisa's famous tower might justifiably lean to the edge of your picture, but a snap of the kids at the seaside, say, with the sea running out of one side of the image, isn't an attractive shot. You can correct problems with leaning photos using iPhoto's Straighten function:

1. Select the picture to straighten.

2. Click Edit.

3. Click Straighten.

4. Move the slider as desired to position the photo.

5. Click Done.

Removing red-eye

Even in an age of super-sensitive digital cameras, flash is a necessary evil of indoor photography, and with flash comes a secondary evil: red-eye. Pets are particularly prone, people less so, but still it happens a lot. Luckily for you, iPhoto makes getting rid of red-eye simple.

Until now, a major problem with digital photography has been in sharing images with your family, friends and colleagues. You can burn a CD, of course, but that means powering up a computer, loading the disk and sitting in front of a monitor, and that's not exactly the experience anyone is looking for these days. It's much the same story hooking up your camera to a TV to watch a slide show of pictures. It's just not that easy – you need the proper cables, to select a TV input and perform other technical tasks. And you know as well as I do that viewing pictures on someone's phone or tiny digital camera screen is really just a nuisance. Finally, while a physical photo album might be old hat, it's survived for so long precisely because it's user-friendly – well, minus the part about you having to print every photo. Photo albums are nice, though; you can thumb through images in a sort of photo slide show.

Apple has tried to reinvent the physical photo album on the computer and has made it pretty easy to create a slide show of your favourite pictures. The slide show mimics the physical photo album option, making it easy to 'flip through' photos you want to share. You can enhance the slide show, too, with effects and transitions, music and other items. Beyond slide shows, though, you have built-in options to order prints, upload photos to your Gallery if you're a subscriber, upload to Flickr or Facebook, or email pictures to others.

Share photos

9

Share photos (cont.)

Share photos in an email

You can select a single photo or multiple photos from inside the iPhoto interface to email it. You can't email video. iPhoto integrates nicely with other apps and the apps can share their information (in this case, contacts). Once you've opted to email a photo (or photos), you'll have many of the features Mail has to offer, too, including choosing a theme, setting a photo size, inserting text and formatting it.

1. Select a picture to email, or hold down the Command key while selecting multiple pictures.

2. Click Share and click Email.

3. Choose a theme in the right pane, if you wish.

4. Type a message.

5. Configure picture size, if desired.

6. Complete the email and click Send.

To create a slide show of your favourite pictures, you first need to group them together. One way to do this is to create an album and put your favourite pictures in it. Once you've populated your new album with images, you can use those to create a slide show. Another option (although there are more than these) is to choose an *event* folder that already exists and create a slide show using the photos there.

To create an album and add photos to it:

1. Select a single photo you'd like to include in your new album.

2. Click File>New>Album.

3. Name the album. It will have only one photo in it.

4. Click Photos, and drag any other photos to the new album.

5. If you have an event folder you'd like to add, drag it to the new album. Every photo in there will be added.

6. Continue adding images as desired.

Once you've created an album (or selected one) that contains your favourite photos, you're ready to create a slide show. To get started, click the album to use, click Create and click Slideshow. With that done, you can name the slide show and begin editing it. If you think you'd just like to view it as is, click Play.

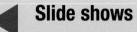

Slide shows

?

Did you know?

You can lower the zoom slider so you can see lots of photos, then click and drag with the mouse to select large groups of images at once. You can then drag all of these to the new album.

9

?

Did you know?

When you can see the Play button, you can also see options to enhance the slide show by adding text slides, applying themes, adding music and more.

Slide shows (cont.)

Edit a slide show

1. Select the slide show you've created in the left pane of iPhoto.

2. Click Themes and select one. Click Choose.

3. Click Preview to see if you like it; choose a different theme if you wish. (Click the iPhoto window to stop the preview.)

4. Click the slides across the top of the iPhoto interface. Stop when Text Slide is an option across the bottom.

5. Input any subtitle text as desired.

6. Click Music.

7. Select a song from the list and click Choose. (Note you can browse for additional music files.)

8. Click Settings.

9. Review the options, including the option to fit the slide show to the music or select a transition to play between slides.

10. Close the Settings page.

11. Click Preview.

12. Continue editing as desired.

You can do a lot more with your slide show than simply show pictures on the screen. You can name it anything you like and include that name on the first slide of the show, add slides that contain your own text, select from various themes to change the look of each slide in the show, add music from your music library and configure how long to play each slide for. You can see the options in the image above, including Text Slide, Themes, Music and Settings.

You can print your pictures using a printer you own by clicking Print from the File menu (or using the Command + P key combination). You can also order prints from Apple. This option is also under File and the command is Order Prints. You can select multiple photos prior to selecting either command to simplify things.

If you select multiple photos and then opt to order prints from Apple, you'll be able to see the pricing, select quantity and size, and pay with the credit card you have on file for iTunes and the App Store. It's about as easy as it can get; in fact, the interface is nearly foolproof and shipping rates and prices are reasonable. If you opt to print from your own printer, you'll have the opportunity to configure printer properties and preferences before you click the Print button. These settings are generally unique to your printer and include the ability to select a paper type and size, print in low or high quality, and similar options.

iPhoto offers its own options too. One of these is to print a contact sheet. You can also opt for various mats, shown here. If you click Customize, you'll have access to even more options, including the ability to apply colour to the mat you select. Here, I've selected to apply dots as a background.

Since there's not much to printing except to click File and click Print, and then perhaps click Customize to choose a background colour, etc., and because printer properties and preferences are unique to the kind of printer you own, I'll leave printing to you. To get started though, remember to click File and Print – the rest will be self-explanatory.

Print

9

For your information

Purchase photo paper for your printer. You'll notice a big difference in the quality and feel of the photos you print.

View videos

You may have noticed that you have videos mixed in with your photos in iPhoto. You can tell an image is a video because it has a small video camera icon in the bottom left corner. See whether you can make out the icon in this image.

View a video in iPhoto

1 Locate the video.

2 Double-click the video to play it.

3 Move your mouse over the video to show the controls.

4 Use the controls to rewind, pause, fast forward, change the volume and more.

When a video is selected in iPhoto, you have options across the bottom just as you do when a photo is selected. Info is selected here. With Info selected, you can type a title and description easily. You can also share the video if you have online accounts in places such as Facebook and Flickr.

You really can't edit a video in iPhoto; iPhoto was made for photos, not videos. You can work with video in iMovie though, something you'll learn about in Chapter 10. For now, the two things you'll be able to do and probably want to do are to view the video and perhaps shorten it.

Shorten a video

Quite a bit of the time, the video you shoot with a digital camera, phone or similar device is longer than it needs to be. You may have to film for 2 or 3 minutes before you get your dog to shake hands or play dead; likewise, you may have filmed way past the optimal time to stop, perhaps because you were waiting for something to happen that didn't. All of this down time reduces the quality of the video and causes viewers to lose interest. It is best to cut out the boring parts, especially if you plan to send the video to a website like Facebook or Flickr. (The shorter the better when it comes to uploading to a website, for the most part anyway.)

Most of the time all you really need to do is cut a bit from the beginning and cut a bit more from the end, and there's no need to drag out iMovie or a complex third-party app to help you do that. It's more common to need to cut from the beginning – most people are pretty good about not filming any more after the desired event has occurred. Either way, to shorten the beginning and end of a video using iPhoto:

1. Double-click the video.

2. When it starts to play, click Pause.

3. Click the Action button.

4. Click Trim.

5. Drag the slider on the left side to the place in the video you'd like it to start.

6. Drag the slider on the right side to the place in the video you'd like it to end.

9

Important

iPhoto doesn't offer much in the way of video editing, but it does offer the option to trim a video. When you trim a video you remove parts of it you don't want.

View videos (cont.)

Communicate with video

There are lots of options for communicating over the Internet with audio, text and/or video, and your Mac offers two distinct options built in. One is iChat, an application that's been around a long time and is compatible with various chat programs; the other is FaceTime, a brand new application that works only with other i-devices, such as other Macs with FaceTime, the iPhone 4 and the iPad 2.

As you'd guess, there are requirements for communicating. With iChat, the user you want to communicate with must have a connection to the Internet and a MobileMe, AIM, Google Talk or Jabber account (and you will too). They'll have to be logged in as well and available for a chat. With FaceTime, the user you want to communicate with must have some device capable of running FaceTime and a connection to the Internet through a Wi-Fi network (as will you). As with iChat, you'll have to be available.

Depending on what you want to do, you may have to install required hardware. For audio conversations only, you'll need a microphone and speakers, or better yet a headset with a microphone built in. If you want to video chat, you'll need a webcam. If you only want to send text messages, you'll simply need a keyboard. If you need to perform any installations before you continue, do so now. However, your Mac may come with all you need – most Macs these days include a webcam and microphone, and all come with speakers for sound.

For your information

Webcams are simple to set up and configure. If you purchase a webcam that's Mac-compatible, all you have to do is connect it and perhaps install something from an accompanying CD.

To use iChat, you need some kind of account to log in with. If you have a MobileMe account, that will certainly do, but if you don't want to pay for an account consider one from AOL, Google or Jabber. Once you have that account, you can open iChat and input the information. With that done, you're ready to chat with others who use compatible programs and who have added you as a friend, contact or buddy. (If you're unsure how to get a free account, visit *www.aol.com*, *www.google.com* or *register.jabber.org* and locate a link to 'create an account'.) If you don't have any account, let me suggest a Google account. Google accounts are user-friendly, work with iChat and can be accessed from almost anywhere.

Account Setup

iChat supports me.com, Mac.com, AIM, Yahoo!, Google Talk, and Jabber accounts.

Account Type: Google Talk
Account Name: joliballew@gmail.com
Password: ••••••••

Cancel   Done

Once you've logged in with your own account, you have to add the people you want to chat with. You have to send an invitation and they have to receive that invitation and agree to be your 'buddy'. There are lots of ways to add buddies (and send invitations). You can click Buddies on the menu bar, click Add Buddy and input the information manually. You can click the + sign in the iChat Buddies window to open this window as well. The only thing you really have to get right here is the account name. If you have more than one account configured for yourself, you have to choose the one to associate the new buddy with from the drop-down list. Then you can type any first and last name and add the contact to the proper buddy list, as applicable.

Set up and use iChat

Setting up iChat

1 Open iChat from the Dock.

2 If you aren't prompted to enter your account information:

   a. Click File and click Preferences.

   b. Click the Accounts tab.

   c. Click the + sign to add a new account, if applicable.

   d. Select the account type and input your user name and password.

3 If you are prompted for account information, follow the prompts to input it.

4 Click Done.

5 Add any additional accounts, if you wish.

9

Set up and use iChat (cont.)

Use iChat

1. Make sure your status is configured to 'available' or another option besides Offline or any version of Away.

2. From any buddy list, double-click the person you want to communicate with.

3. Enter your message in the field at the foot of the Chat window and press Return.

4. Repeat the process to reply when your buddy responds.

5. If you see a phone icon or a video icon by your contact's name, click it to send audio or audio/video.

If the buddy is already in your Address Book, you don't have to type the information manually – just click the down arrow by the Last name option and additional information will appear. From there, select the buddy to add. Here, I'm adding Mrs. Washington.

Once you've added buddies and they've accepted your invitation, you can use iChat to communicate with them. You'll see that buddies have been added in the iChat window. If you don't see any window, click iChat in the Dock, then click Window from the menu bar. Select the account to view. If you're using Jabber, for instance, you'll want Jabber to have a tick beside it.

6 Wait while the buddy responds.

7 Communicate as desired, speaking and gesturing as you feel like it.

9

Important !

There can be issues when video chatting with others who aren't also using iChat because some chat clients aren't fully compatible. However, it works quite often and you'll be notified if it won't.

For your information ⓘ

You can't just send video, audio or text to anyone. Imagine what a mess that would be! When you opt to send video, even to a buddy, that buddy has to want to see you. Thus, you may have to wait for the buddy to respond, as applicable.

Set up and use FaceTime

Did you know?

FaceTime is a free app and it's available from the App Store.

Did you know?

iPad 2, iPhone 4 and iPod Touch users must be connected to a Wi-Fi network to use FaceTime.

FaceTime lets you hold audio/video chats with others. The people you want to video chat with must have an iPad 2, iPhone 4, iPod Touch or a Mac with a video camera, and FaceTime must be installed and set up on that device. *You* must have a webcam installed and be connected to the Internet, and you must also perform a few set-up tasks. Once both you and your contact are ready, only then can you communicate via FaceTime. It's easy to tell if a contact is ready and available – you will see a video camera by their name.

Although it may seem like quite a lot to do to make FaceTime work, it really isn't. FaceTime is much easier to set up and use than iChat and other video-conferencing software for lots of reasons. For one, it's not buggy because you'll communicate only with people who also have FaceTime. Second, you simply input your email address to get started. Finally, incompatible software, chat clients, multiple chat accounts, etc. aren't an issue. To top it off, the FaceTime video you send and receive is crisp and clear, and the controls are easy to find and use.

To set up FaceTime:

1. From the Applications window, open FaceTime.

2. Sign in with your Apple ID or opt to create a new account.

3. Type or select the email account to use to be notified of FaceTime calls and click Next.

4. You must now locate a contact from your contact list to communicate with, or add a new contact. One way is to:

   a. Click Contacts in the FaceTime window.

   b. Click the + sign in the All Contacts list.

   c. Type the desired information.

   d. Click Done.

Once you've set up FaceTime with your Apple ID and password, and configured an email address to use for invitations, all you need to do is to locate the contact in your contact list and initiate the call. Of course, the person you want to call has to be online and available, so you may want to contact them ahead of time and let them know when you'll be calling, but other than that it's pretty easy.

1. Open FaceTime.

2. If necessary, log in.

3. Click Favorites, Recents or Contacts to locate the person to video chat with.

4. If the user has a video camera by their name, click it to start the video call.

5. To end the call, click End.

Set up and use FaceTime (cont.)

9

For your information

When in Contacts, select a contact and click Add to Favorites. Then the contact will also be available from the Favorites option.

Important

You can't send someone video of yourself without their permission. If you are having trouble making a call to a person, make sure they know you're trying to call them via FaceTime and let them know when you'll be calling.

iMovie, iDVD, GarageBand and iWeb

Introduction

You have lots of iApps on your Mac, including iPhoto, iChat, iCal and iTunes. You've learned about these apps in this book. There are more iApps to discover though, including iMovie, iDVD and iWeb, and one last straggler without the familiar i, GarageBand. You'll use these apps to create, manipulate, view and publish digital material in the form of images, movie clips, music and online content.

Your familiarity with iTunes and iPhoto will help you become adapt with these apps quickly. There are a lot of similarities in the interfaces. As you'd guess, each app will have a menu bar with menu titles and options that you've seen before, they will enable you to browse your computer for the files you need, and each will offer familiar save and editing options. Keep in mind as you read this chapter that entire books have been written on GarageBand, as well as on iWeb and iMovie. Thus, what you learn here will be just enough to get you started. If you think you'd like to learn more, you'll find plenty of resources at Apple's website, bookstores and in online discussion sites dedicated to the app.

What you'll do

Explore iMovie

Create a basic movie with iMovie

Explore iDVD

Burn a DVD with iDVD

Explore GarageBand

Mix music with GarageBand

Explore iWeb

Create a basic web page with iWeb

Create a movie with iMovie ▶

Once upon a time, making movies was impossibly high-tech (or low-tech, depending on how you see it). You needed a specialised camera, specialised film and some kind of processing studio. You had to meticulously edit your work using specific tools that very few people knew how to use. Those tools were expensive, too. As time passed, digital video cameras became mainstream and people began to record video regularly; unfortunately, the software that was required to edit what was recorded was anything but straightforward. For the most part, what happened in those early days was that you simply offered to your audience whatever video was shot with the camera. There was very little editing and certainly no transitions, credits or introductions. Now, there's iMovie. With iMovie, Apple iLife's digital video-editing suite, you can create real movies, just like the ones you see in the cinema, and you don't need £1 million and a PhD to use it.

You might find the icon for iMovie in the Dock. If you've moved it, you'll have to look in the Applications folder. Once opened, you'll see a Welcome screen, a prompt and various panes, shown here. Click Now to let iMovie set itself up.

You'll notice that the Welcome screen encourages you to get started by working through some step-by-step lessons. I strongly encourage you to do this. You can find the lessons from Help>iMovie Help. Here, Lesson 2 is playing (I've opted to view it in Safari) and it's entitled Start a new project. Each video is about 2 minutes long, so it should take you only about 15 minutes to view all seven videos.

You'll notice as you get to know iMovie that the interface is similar to iPhoto. You can skim thumbnail previews of video clips imported from your video camera, there's a menu bar with options, and you can drag and drop images to group them. Just like iPhoto, iMovie imports, organises and stores video as events, which is a convenient label that assumes that the video

Explore iMovie through video

1　Open iMovie.

2　Click Help>iMovie Help.

3　Click Import video.

4　Read what's offered. Then, under Watch the movie, click the movie title.

5　If the movie doesn't play automatically, click Open with Safari.

6　Watch the movie.

10

Get to know iMovie (cont.)

you're importing is associated with a particular date and event, such as a birthday or footage from a concert you attended.

As well as importing, storing, organising and previewing your clips, you can create movies by dragging and dropping sections of imported source material into a project, preview and edit to get it just right, then share your movie on YouTube, export it to your iPod, iPhone or iPad, or watch it on your Apple TV, among other things.

Import raw video

Before you can use iMovie, you'll have to film some video using your digital video camera. Additionally, you must be able to get the video off the camera and onto your Mac. This means that your video camera must be Mac-compatible, or if not, there must be some way to import the raw footage, such as pulling it off a camera's SD card if applicable.

If you're not sure whether or not your camera is supported, click Help, and click Supported Cameras. From there, you can select a device type, manufacturer, format, type of media, even your regional settings. Alternatively, you connect your camera, turn it on, set it to Playback or Computer, and see whether your Mac recognises it.

If, for whatever reason, you don't have any raw video of your own, you can import video from other sources. If you've used iMovie before, you can click File>Import and select the appropriate option to locate your previous iMovie project. You can also import QuickTime movies direct from your hard drive or clips from video-enabled still cameras from the iPhoto video library. To see what's available to you, click File>Import>Movies.

For your information

If iMovie won't recognise your camcorder or digital video camera, make sure it's connected to the correct port. Cameras that record to flash, HDD or DVD connect to a USB port; cameras that record on DV or HDV tape connect with a FireWire port.

Edit footage

Import video into iMovie and very quickly you'll begin to build the perfect library and a super-convenient backup of your most precious filmed moments. You can browse and organise as easily as launching the application; no more afternoons in the dark struggling with an overheating projector or fiddling with an analogue camcorder, a sea of cables and an unresponsive television. What's more, with footage on your Mac, you can make real movies! It's time to get creative – you can select and edit clips at will, create movies and share them with others. You'll be surprised at what iMovie has to offer, including transitions, text pages, music and more.

To get started, you need to select the clips you want to add to your project. You do that by dragging and dropping them from the bottom pane to the top. By default, the Project files are shown on top and the imported files on the bottom. There's a small two-arrow icon next to the zoom slider near the middle of the iMovie interface that lets you switch this to its opposite.

?

Did you know?

You can use File>Import>Movies to pull movies from a connected SD card.

Import raw video

1 Start iMovie and connect your camera.

2 Set the camera to the playback, computer or connect mode, as applicable.

3 If your camcorder uses physical tapes, connecting it will launch an import window complete with camera controls so that you can play, rewind and fast forward the tape in the camera.

4 If your camera stores video on flash cards, HD or DVD, video appears automatically as individual clips in the Import Window.

5 Click any clip and press the space bar to play it.

6 If your camera isn't recognised, click File>Import. Select Movies and browse to the video. You can also click Camera Archive if you don't find the video you want.

7 Look in the section entitled Event Library. Select iPhoto Videos to see what's already on your Mac.

8 Use the slider to make the clips appear larger in the preview window.

10

Get to know iMovie (cont.)

Select the clips for your first project

1. Click in the clip to add, and drag the slider to the place you'd like the video to start.

2. Drag the other end of the slider to the place where you'd like the clip to end.

3. Drag the clip to the top section of iMovie.

4. Click the Play button in the Project window to preview your movie.

Once you've added some clips, you can add other elements. Under the window that shows the preview of the selected clip are various icons. Those icons are shown here. In the image below, I've clicked the T, for theme (or text slide). Note the slides that can be added. Select one and drag it to a place in your project file. Consider dragging the first one to the beginning of your video. Now you can type a title for your project and click Done. Add slides as desired. You can create a title slide, a credits slide, an intermission slide, and slides in between different events to let viewers know to expect a new movie file.

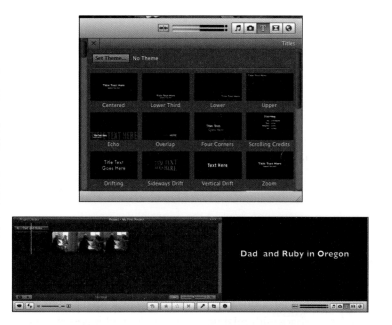

As you continue to explore, you'll find other items you can add. One is a transition. Let's say you are creating a movie that details all the things you did on holiday. Perhaps you did some camping, some mountain climbing, some river rafting. You can import the clips, then separate them with title slides and finally separate those with transitions. A transition comes in many flavours: there's Ripple, Fade to Black (a good one for ending a movie), Mosaic, Slide Left, Puzzle Right, and more.

Continue editing and explore sound effects like Animals, Jingles and Sci-Fi. Note that you can also select music from your music library. You can click the Picture icon next to Themes and add still pictures, too. You can keep an eye on the length of your movie in the status bar that runs across the bottom of the screen, and you can explore many more features from the menu bar. One of those menu titles is Share, where you can share to iDVD, iTunes, CNN iReport, and more. This is where you'll export your movie, too, where you'll save it with its own name, choose where to save and choose a quality.

Make the movie

You can preview your movie at any time in the creation process by clicking the Play button. You can also use the space bar to play your movie. And you can set movie preferences – for instance, from the File menu, you can select Project Properties to set the aspect ratio (Widescreen 16:9 or Standard 4:3). When you're ready to complete your movie, click File>Finalize Project. Wait while iMovie turns your raw footage into a movie. When it's complete, you'll be ready to share the movie with others.

Although there are many ways to share your movie once it's finalised, an easy way is to show it with iDVD. Then you can use iDVD to create a physical DVD of your creation. This offers a nice way to back up your movie to physical media, make copies to share with relatives and friends, and if you choose this option, it provides an easy segue into the next section (which covers iDVD).

Get to know iMovie (cont.)

Add a transition

1 Click the Transition icon. It's next to the Themes icon shown in the previous image.

2 Drag any transition to any area in the Project timeline and drop it there.

3 Repeat as desired.

10

Get to know iMovie (cont.)

Share a movie with iDVD

1 Click Share>iDVD. Notice the other sharing options while you're here.

2 When iDVD opens, minimise iMovie.

3 Click the title of your movie in the iDVD window and rename it if you wish.

4 Double-click the title to play it.

As you can guess, there is a lot more you can do with iMovie than we introduced in this short section. Entire books have been written on using iMovie. You can make professional-looking videos and share them with others in many ways. If this little teaser has you wanting more, there are plenty of additional resources out there for you.

If your Mac has a recordable DVD drive, you can use iDVD to burn your own movie DVDs, slide shows, presentations and music with animated backdrops of still images, among other things. You record these to blank or rewritable DVDs that can be played in standard domestic DVD players or in a computer. You can choose from iDVD's comprehensive selection of predesigned themes and drag-and-drop video, music and images from other iApps, such as iMovie, iTunes and GarageBand, too. You can also easily burn a DVD of a movie you've created in iMovie.

Burn a DVD of an iMovie

1. Open iDVD.
2. Click Create a New Project.
3. Name the DVD, set other options as desired and click Create.
4. Click File>OneStep DVD from Movie.
5. Locate the movie you created in the previous section. (Look in the Movies folder, under iMovie Projects.)
6. Double-click the movie to import.
7. Insert a writable DVD into the recordable DVD drive.
8. Wait while the movie is burned.

10

Explore iDVD

I prefer to create a movie with iMovie and then burn the movie with iDVD because I'm pretty comfortable with iMovie (as you may be by now). However, you can use iDVD to create DVDs directly, using clips you have stored on your computer or a camera. However, until you become familiar with the application and develop confidence using its features, consider using iDVD's assistant – it's called Magic DVD.

To get started, click File>Magic DVD. You'll have the opportunity to type a name for the new DVD, choose a theme and drag and drop movies and photos, even add background music. You'll use this in a similar manner to iMovie. It's really all about locating the media and dragging and dropping it to the desired area. For now, type a name and select a theme.

Add video using Magic DVD

Once you've decided on a theme, you can begin to add video, photos, music and other content, and customise menus and buttons. As you can see from the image opposite, you can access media in the right pane and drag it to the desired position on the Movies or Photos timeline. Note the tabs; here, Movies is selected. I've already dragged two video clips to the Movies area.

For your information

If you want to add photos, make sure you click the Photos tab first. To add audio, click the Audio tab first.

To preview the movie, click the Preview button in the bottom left corner. If you like your creation, click Create Project. This will finalise your project and offer access to additional tools you'll need to use to finish your DVD, such as the Project Info option, detailed next.

Burn a DVD

Before burning a DVD, select Project Info from the Project menu and choose from the various options to ensure your DVD will be suitable for the purpose intended. You can encode the DVD in the American NTSC format if you plan to send it to a friend or relative in the US, for instance. From the Encoding pop-up menu, you can trade speed against space, too. Best Performance is swift, but larger projects will require a more comprehensive, complex and therefore slower encoding process. Monitor the Capacity gauge and choose an encoding strategy to suit the available resources. Close this window when you've finished here.

Burn a Magic DVD

1 Insert a blank DVD and click the Burn button (iDVD will prompt for a disk if you haven't yet inserted one).

2 iDVD displays a progress dialogue showing the various stages of rendering and encoding before burning the disk.

3 After burning, iDVD ejects the finished DVD ready for watching on any suitable player or computer.

10

Explore GarageBand

▶

GarageBand is the iLife application that transforms your Mac into a personal recording studio complete with multi-track mixer, recorder and sampled instruments. Serious musicians and budding sound engineers can use the truly immense scope and power of GarageBand to record the next Top 20 hit or award-winning movie theme. For the rest of us, there's Magic GarageBand, a built-in wizard that will help any non-musician to put together fun music tracks to impress themselves, friends and family.

Understand GarageBand features

GarageBand's icon is in the Dock and in the Applications folder. Click the icon to launch the application. The introductory screen can help you learn to play the guitar or piano, start a new project with Magic GarageBand (and learn about GarageBand features in the process), and even create a personalised ringtone for your iPhone.

You can also access training videos. As with iMovie, there are videos to help you get started and to create a simple project. You can watch videos that teach you how to create a project, take a music lesson, record your voice, play and record your own electric guitar, add loops, add effects, and more. You can even send your song to iTunes if you create something you'd like to share with others. To access this screen, click Help>GarageBand Help. As with iMovie, I strongly suggest you watch these videos before continuing here.

10

Let's start by creating a project and exploring the controls:

1. Open GarageBand and click File>New.

2. Name your new project in the Save As field, make a mental note of the other options and then click Create.

3. The GarageBand editing screen is displayed and there's one instrument, the Grand Piano, in the tracks section. Also displayed is the virtual keyboard. You can use this to enter musical notes by clicking the piano keys. Enter a few notes by playing them on your keyboard.

4. For this exercise, you'll use pre-recorded loops, so for now click the virtual keyboard's Close icon to remove it from the screen. It's the red X located on the virtual piano's top left corner.

5. Click Track and Show Track Info. Under Software Instrument, click Electric Piano from the pane on the right.

6. Click the Loop Browser toggle. It's located in the bottom right corner of the GarageBand interface. It's blue here and looks like a loop. The Loops pane appears.

7. Click Electric Piano and locate Moody Electric Piano 01. Drag and drop this loop to the middle pane. Position it at the beginning of the timeline.

8. Repeat to add Moody Electric Piano 03, but this time hold down the Option key while dragging. Position this a little later in the timeline.

Explore GarageBand (cont.)

9. Now press the Play button to listen to the two bars of music you've just created. Press Play again to stop playback.

10. Finally, rewind the playhead to the start by clicking the Jump to beginning button.

Although this is a simple introduction, with only two loops, it gives you a feel for GarageBand and how you can use it to create your own music. Continue to experiment with different instruments and explore the various views in the Loops pane.

Once you start to become more familiar with GarageBand, you'll see the immense scope of the application. Like real-world multi-track recorders, GarageBand can be used to record instruments, voices, drumbeats, etc. as separate tracks, which are mixed together to create a song. Each track is displayed horizontally across the GarageBand window. Tracks have a number of controls and you can choose from various musical scales including Minor, Major, Neither or Good For Both.

At the left of a track you can see the name of the instrument that recorded the track along with a number of controls. To the right there's the mixer section, which you use to adjust panning (whether sounds come from the right or left of the stereo mix) and playback volume. Use the disclosure triangle at the right of the Tracks section to hide and reveal the mixer. To the right of the mixer is a visualisation of the recording.

Recordings are created with loops – individual blocks of recorded sound – placed on a timeline divided into measures (numbered) and beats (vertical indicators between the measure numbers). Loops can be pre-recorded (many are shipped with GarageBand), acquired from the Web or recorded live from an instrument or voice. You can place a loop anywhere on the timeline and copy and repeat it.

In the toolbar at the bottom of the editing screen, there are buttons to add a new track, toggle the track editor, familiar DVD-like controls for record, playback, rewind, fast forward and so on, a digital counter (click to jump directly to measures, beats or a relative time in your song), master volume (the overall volume of the tracks in the project), track info and media browser buttons.

Explore GarageBand (cont.)

?

Did you know?

The playhead is the point at which the music starts to play. Click in the timeline to position the playhead.

10

Mix your music

Once you've added tracks you can add more tracks and then concentrate on mixing your music. In your simple piano project, you may opt to add a bass guitar. Consider adding Alternative Rock Bass 04 to measure 1 below the existing tracks.

You could continue to add tracks such as Alternative Rock Bass 03 to a different measure, or Alternative Rock Bass 04 somewhere else. There are key combinations that enable you to perform tasks too. For instance, to move multiple tracks, you can Shift + click all the piano loops and then drag them to a new part of the timeline. Continue exploring as desired and when you've added a few tracks that seem to sound good together you'll be ready to continue.

The last stage in the music-making process is to mix your masterpiece. Mixing is the art of balancing the position and volume of the various tracks until they sound just right. Here are a few mixing techniques to try:

■ Rotate a track's rotary control to pan music so that it is positioned predominantly to the left or the right of the stereo mix. Panning brings life to your music, giving it a dramatic tension that attracts the ear and catches the attention. It also separates elements that might otherwise fight with each other and muddy the sound.

■ Begin with the percussion tracks (drums, followed by shakers and so on), adjusting the volume, so that there's plenty of power but without breaking up the quality of the sound. Mute all the other tracks (click the headphones button to solo the track you're working with). As you bring up the volume, watch the volume indicators for left and right stereo channels so that the volume peaks at about the midway point.

■ Adjust the volume for the bass so that it's balanced with the drums and can be heard clearly without being overly prominent.

■ Adjust the melody instruments, the guitar, piano and so on, in proportion with the bass and drums, and according to your ears and what you're trying to achieve with the song.

■ Now enable all tracks and listen to your project. If some tracks seem to be competing with others, causing the sound to be muddied, pan them left and right to give the project breathing space. Try to keep the bass and drums in the centre of the mix or panned only very gently left or right of centre.

10

Share your music

Create an MP3 of your song

1. Click Share>Export Song to Disk.
2. Choose MP3 from the Compress Using pop-up menu.
3. Click Export.
4. Name the song, choose where to save it and click Save.

When your project sounds as it should, it's time to let others hear it! GarageBand perfectly integrates with iApps such as iTunes, iDVD and iWeb to enable you to share your tunes, burn them to a CD and publish them on the Web.

To export a project to your iTunes library, select Send Song to iTunes from the Share menu. Complete the various fields for artist, composer, album and so on. Select AAC Encoder from the Compress Using pop-up menu. Click Share.

Send your song to your iTunes library.

iTunes Playlist: Joli Ballew's Playlist
Artist Name: Joli Ballew
Composer Name: Joli Ballew
Album Name: Joli Ballew's Album

☑ Compress

Compress Using: AAC Encoder
Audio Settings: Medium Quality

Ideal for music of all types. Download times are moderate. Details: AAC, 128kbps, Stereo, optimized for music and complex audio. Estimated Size: 0.3MB.

Cancel   Share

GarageBand will now mix down a final take according to your track and mixing settings and save it to the iTunes library. iTunes is launched and the song plays automatically. If further editing is required, return to GarageBand, tweak the project and Send Song again.

There are more ways to share. You can send a ringtone to iTunes, send a podcast you've created to iWeb, send a movie to iDVD, and export the song to a disk. You can even burn the song to a CD to share it with others anywhere, anytime. You can also mix down a project as a standard MP3 to play on a compatible digital music player, or to copy to your phone for use as a ringtone.

If you don't have your own piece of the Internet pie, you'd probably like to. You have Facebook, Google + and Windows Live, but you probably don't have your own web page. With your own web page (or website), you get to decide every element, every icon, and your page can be ad-free. You can decide which hyperlinks to include, what content to show, and you can use your web page to blog daily, post information about your company's products, or even set up a calendar to share family activities. There are lots of reasons to create your own web page, even if they are temporary ones.

Explore the iWeb interface

To launch the iWeb application, click its icon in the Applications folder. The application is designed to integrate perfectly with other iApps, such as iMovie, iPhoto and GarageBand (for podcasts), and you'll notice similarities in the interface.

When you build a web page (or a website), you include various elements such as pictures, text, video clips and clickable links to other parts of your site and external web pages. iWeb's strength lies in providing attractive templates for your pages, which are predesigned to suit all kinds of online publishing needs. To create an attractive and interactive website, all you need to do is select a template and customise it with your own content. The days of writing HTML to create a simple web page are long gone, so there's no programming required.

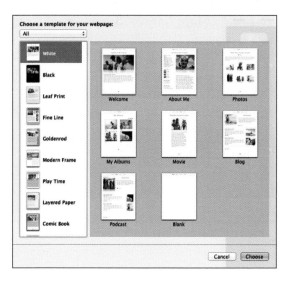

Create a web page with iWeb

Important

You'll have to pay someone to host your web page or website. Creating it will be free, but hosting it will incur a monthly fee. If you add email to the package, you'll have to pay extra as well.

! 10

Create a web page with iWeb (cont.)

Add an image to a web page

1. Verify that the Media pane is showing. The Media icon should show Hide Media when this is the case.

2. From the Media pane, note the tabs: Audio, Photos, Movies and Widgets. Click Photos.

3. Locate the photo to add.

4. Drag the photo to any photo placeholder.

To select a theme, simply browse through the options, click the one you like and click Choose. To start, if applicable, click the Welcome screen template page. This will let you focus on what your page will be about and will help you decide whether you'd like to include other pages as well.

Build your page

Now the fun starts! Select a placeholder, either text or image, and replace it with your own information. You can restyle text using the Format menu. You can also click and drag page elements to new locations. As you build, explore these options for customising the template you've selected:

■ To select text for editing, double-click it or click and then click again to place a cursor in the text, scrolling to select the text you want to change. The text is highlighted and you can type over it.

■ While the text is selected, choose a font (Format>Font>Show Fonts), size (Format>Font>Bigger/ Smaller) and style (Format>Font>Bold/Italic, etc.) from the Format menu.

■ Align selected text by choosing centred, justified and so on from the Format>Text menu.

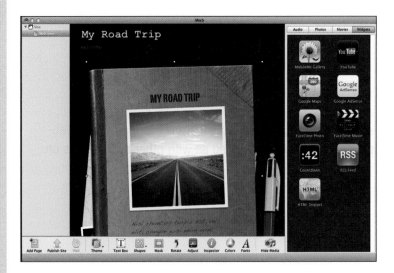

You'll notice as you work that text is contained within invisible boxes that can be relocated to suit your requirements. To tweak the location of a text box, click and drag it. You can move an element when you have access to the small white squares, shown opposite. You can also add text boxes by clicking the Text Box icon in the toolbar at the foot of the Preview window.

Once you've got the text in order you can start working on the images. Depending on the template you choose, the placeholders available for displaying photos vary. However, you can drag a photo on a page even if there's not a placeholder there. You can resize too, simply by dragging from the corners of any selected image.

After you've added photos, click a photo and then click the Edit Mask button to alter the way the image is cropped and to determine the size of the reflection effect. Note that you can also add audio and video to your web page, as well as widgets. Widgets include the MobileMe Gallery, YouTube, Google Maps, FaceTime Photo and more.

Continue editing until you have your Welcome page just the way you want it. Then click Add Page at the bottom of the iWeb interface. Choose another page and edit it as you wish. Continue until your entire website is complete.

As you explore more, look under each of the iWeb menus. For instance, under Insert you can insert a hyperlink (that's a link to another web page), a text box, a shape, button or widget. Under the Arrange menu you can select an item to move it to the back so that it's behind other elements, or to the front so that it's on top of other elements. There are also iWeb preferences you can set, and as with other applications on your Mac, you'll be able to set options. When you think your web page is ready, click File and click Publish Entire Site.

Create a web page with iWeb (cont.)

?

Did you know?

You can easily replace one image with another by dragging a new photo to any photo placeholder. You can also select a photo and click Delete on the keyboard to remove it.

10

Upload options

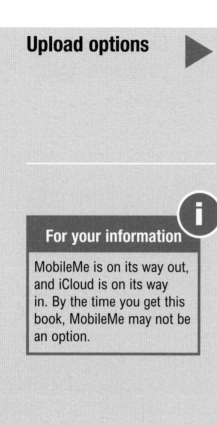

For your information

MobileMe is on its way out, and iCloud is on its way in. By the time you get this book, MobileMe may not be an option.

No one will be able to access your web page or website from the Internet until you publish it. To publish, you'll have to pay a company to 'host' your website so others can access it. Hosting companies abound, and these companies will store your files, make them available on the Internet, and will often offer other services, such as providing you with an email address, helping you get your website placed on various search engine sites, and will back up your data regularly.

One way to publish your web page is to use a MobileMe account. This is a service, provided by Apple, that you pay for. Uploading your site is one of the features of MobileMe and with it you can easily publish websites, blogs and photo pages, and upload changes as you make them. This is the easiest option. You can use MobileMe free for 60 days if you'd like to try it out. If you decide to do this, just click File>Publish Entire Site and follow the prompts.

If you don't want to use MobileMe, you'll have to find another way to publish your site. You'll need some online storage space for the data you want to upload. You may be able to get that through your ISP, or you may opt for a larger company such as GoDaddy. Depending on the company you choose and their requirements, you may also need an FTP (File Transfer Protocol) client application to upload the data for your website to your storage space. FTP clients are freely available to download from a variety of freeware and shareware sources. Many web-hosting companies offer easy-to-use upload tools and many also offer their own templates. Although I'm not suggesting you use GoDaddy, and I'm simply using the company as an example, GoDaddy does offer options and instructions for uploading your iWeb creations. If you opt for a hosting company other than MobileMe, it will be up to you to learn how to upload and what tools you'll need to do so.

You've almost reached the end of this book, but hopefully not the end of your journey. There are a few things I haven't covered here, including various utilities (in the Applications folder) and applications such as Photo Booth, QuickTime Player, Remote Connection and a few others. You can explore those now, though; what you've learned here will take you a long way and make these applications easier to use. Apple has done a good job of making sure that all of its applications have similar items available from the menu bar, for example, and that you can drag and drop in many instances to format and move data.

There's also the issue of exploring the rest of the System Preferences. Although you've learned about quite a few of the options, there are still more to explore. For instance, the Language & Text option lets you select your preferred language and associate your Mac with it, including how numbers, time and currency are displayed. Universal Access options enable you to set options for using your Mac if you're hearing- or visually-impaired, or if you have trouble typing or using a mouse. Under CDs & DVDs, you can configure what you want to happen when you insert this type of media. You may not want iTunes to open when you insert a music CD if you have another program you prefer. There's more to explore in other options, too. The point is, this book is a jumping-off point, and should you have learned enough here to continue exploring on your own, and with confidence.

Where to go from here

10

Maintenance, security and troubleshooting

Introduction

Almost everything you own must be secured and maintained. You must lock the doors of your home to keep out intruders, change the oil in your car to keep it running properly, and update insurance policies and address books (among other things) to stay up to date. In the same vein, you must also secure, maintain and update your Mac to keep it and the data on it safe, too.

Much of what you will do in this chapter is preventative. For instance, you can configure your Mac so that a password is required to log in, as well as to view the screen after a screen saver has been applied. This keeps out nosy family members and coworkers, and keeps anyone from accidentally installing something on your Mac that could cause it harm. You can also incorporate energy-saving options to make sure your Mac doesn't have to work hard when it doesn't need to, and to lengthen the life of the battery. You can configure various security settings such as enabling the firewall, encrypting with FileVault, and more.

There are lots of things you can do to protect you and your Mac that aren't available as options anywhere on it. This is where common sense comes into play. For instance, you can protect the data on your Mac by ignoring email from people you don't know and logging off when you've finished using your computer. If you travel with a Mac, keep it in the boot of the car and away from extreme heat and cold. There are lots of other ways to protect your Mac:

- Keep your laptop in your sight or locked up at all times when you're away from your desk, at a coffee shop or in another public place.

- Download software from reputable websites only and only after you've researched the software thoroughly.

- Protect external hard drives with encryption and passwords.

- Don't give your passwords to anyone, but do make them available to your children in your will or a safe deposit box they'll have access to should something happen to you.

- Back up data to your iPhone, iPad or iPod if you have one.

- Follow the guidelines in this chapter to further protect your Mac, keep it updated, and learn tips and techniques for troubleshooting your Mac when things go wrong.

You learned the importance of getting software updates early on in this book, in Chapter 1. You learned that getting the updates Apple releases will keep your computer safe by protecting it from newfound security threats and security holes, by applying fixes for bugs and problems with existing components and installed software, and so on. You also learned to configure preferences so that you'd get updates automatically. If you don't remember how to do that, make sure you return to that chapter for a refresher.

There's more to update than just your Mac's OS though. For instance, in Chapter 8 you learned that you should check for updates to iTunes the first time you use it. Later, when prompted, you should opt to install updates for other Apple components, like Safari, QuickTime, GarageBand, etc. There's more to it than that, though. Occasionally you'll be prompted to update programs for your connected hardware, including iPads and printers, and for third-party applications you've installed such as word-processing or photo-editing programs. Often, in third-party apps, you'll find the option to check for updates under the Help menu on the menu bar.

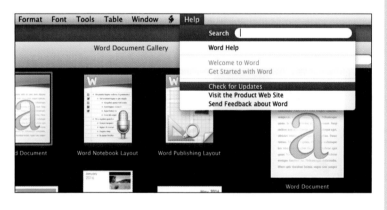

The problem is in knowing what you should update and when, especially when that information comes in the form of a prompt that appears seemingly out of nowhere. On Windows computers, these prompts to update software can be a ruse to get you to register and give up your email address and personal information; other times it can be actually malicious and something that has bypassed your computer's defences. Sometimes, prompts to update something are really a virus working its way into your system and looking for your blessing.

Get software updates (cont.)

The question is, then, how vigilant should you be about prompts you see on your Mac, specifically prompts to update something? That's certainly a valid question, but lucky for you, hackers don't tend to target Mac users. It's highly unlikely that any prompt you see would be malicious unless you were unwittingly installing rogue software or in the process of opening a bad attachment in an email. However, when you are prompted, make sure you recognise the program and the publisher, and make sure you really do need the update and that it's for a program you use regularly. That said, when you see the prompt here, always opt to Show Details, even though you can tell it's from Apple.

Yes, I mentioned the possibility that your Mac could get a virus in the previous section, and indeed it is possible. Although you probably hear all the time that Macs can't get viruses, it's just not true. Macs have fewer threats thrown at them than Windows computers do, but they are not immune. It's important to protect your Mac with anti-virus software, even if your friends and colleagues insist you don't need to.

Before you run out and buy or download and install anti-virus software, though, do your homework. Make sure you explore trusted companies and read reviews of their software. Make sure those reviews are from trusted sites such as CNET, ZDNet, etc. If you are still unsure after researching online, visit a local computer store and ask the salespeople there what they suggest.

◀ **Install an anti-virus program** 11

Download and install anti-virus software

1 Download an anti-virus program you've researched and trust.

2 Work through the installation program, making sure you protect *all users* on the computer.

3 Configure the software as applicable, making sure you create a schedule for scans and updates.

! Important

Some free anti-virus software you'll find on the Web isn't free at all. In fact, it's often a scam to trap you into buying the full version. This software starts off by 'scanning' your Mac and uncovering all kinds of problems, viruses, worms and other threats. Then the only way to get rid of these threats (and the annoying pop-ups you'll see until you do something) is to purchase the full version of the software you've used to scan for them.

! Important

Don't just install any free anti-virus software: do your homework. Make sure you read reviews and user comments and that the software is trusted by professionals.

Explore security options ▶

Enable the Firewall

1 Open System Preferences.

2 Click Security & Privacy.

3 Click the Firewall tab.

4 Click Start.

5 Click Advanced and review the exceptions. For now, leave these as they are if you know you've already enabled sharing with others, but be aware that you can make changes if you need to.

Encrypt with FileVault

1 Click System Preferences>Security & Privacy.

2 Click the FileVault tab.

3 Click Turn On FileVault.

4 Type a master password, verify it and type a hint only you can figure out.

5 Click Continue.

6 Enter your user account password and click OK.

7 Read the information carefully, then click Turn On FileVault (or click Cancel if you've changed your mind).

Your Mac offers a security option in the System Preferences pane. In Lion, the icon is called Security & Privacy. Make sure you click the lock and enter an administrator's name and password before you attempt to make changes here. Once in, there are four tabs available:

■ General – click here to require a password after a screen saver starts, to disable automatic login, to log out after a specific period of inactivity, to show a message when the screen is locked, and more.

■ FileVault – this can be enabled to secure the data on your Mac by encrypting it. FileVault also encrypts the contents of your Home folder. If your computer is stolen and a thief pulls the hard drive, he still won't be able to access your data without your password. You can turn on FileVault if you want the extra protection, but if you lose (or forget) your password, even you won't be able to access the data on it.

❗ Important

You really need to write down your passwords and keep them somewhere, but that 'where' is the big issue. Consider storing your passwords in a locked safe if you have one. Even a locked filing cabinet or an unassuming shoe box in the wardrobe is better than nothing.

- Firewall – the Firewall isn't enabled by default, but you can enable it to limit the types of incoming connections that are allowed. Once enabled, the advanced options let you choose specific programs and features that do have access, such as file and printer sharing, or sharing media through iTunes. The Mac's Firewall can help protect your Mac from unwanted intruders and hackers because when you limit what can access your Mac, you protect it.

- Privacy – click here to send information to Apple to help the company improve its products. No personally identifiable information is sent; your privacy is maintained. You can also turn on or off Location Services, a feature many apps use to learn your location. When enabled, apps can give you accurate directions, information about traffic, the current weather, and more. However, those apps will know where you are if enabled, which may unnerve you.

Explore additional security settings

1 Open System Preferences>Security & Privacy.

2 Click the General tab.

3 Make sure Disable automatic login is ticked (enabled).

4 If desired, select Log out after ___ minutes of inactivity.

5 Click the Privacy tab.

6 To keep your Mac from sharing its location information with websites and applications, select Disable Location Services. (I prefer to leave this enabled.)

7 Click the lock to make sure no changes are made without your permission.

Important !

The lock icon must be unlocked to make changes to the Firewall.

Protect your computer with passwords

The best way to secure your Mac from damage your kids, friends, guests or coworkers can do is to protect it with a strong password. Once it's protected, you can enhance that security by logging off automatically after a specific period of time or configuring a password-protected screen saver, both available from System Preferences and outlined in the previous section. However, you must have a password configured on every account for it to be effective – that's what you'll learn here.

1. Open System Preferences and click Users & Groups (this used to be Accounts).
2. If the lock icon appears locked, you must click it to make changes to any System Preferences options.
3. For every account that does not have a password (or a strong password), click either Change Password or Reset Password, as applicable.
4. Type the new password twice, and type a password hint.
5. Click Reset Password.

Important !

Don't tape your password to the underside of your keyboard tray, mouse pad or desk drawer. Everyone knows that trick!

For your information ⓘ

A strong password contains letters, numbers and symbols, and can include capital letters. If you have a hard time remembering passwords but want to create a strong one, consider one like ILoveMy2CatZ or MyMacRock$2012.

Important !

Do you see the option above to set parental controls? Consider this for accounts you configure for your children.

Once you have configured a password for your account, you can enable a screen saver to appear after a specific period of idle time that you set. You can then require that a password be entered to bring the Mac out of screen-saver mode. This will protect your Mac from prying eyes and also keep visitors from stopping by and installing software or causing harm to your Mac after it's been idle for a while.

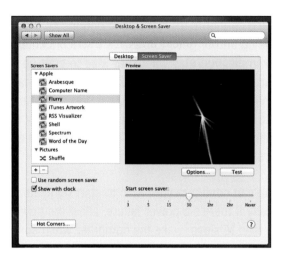

Protect with a screen-saver password

1 Click System Preferences>Desktop & Screen Saver.

2 Click the Screen Saver tab and select any screen saver.

3 Configure how long to wait until the screen saver is applied.

4 Click Show All.

5 Click Security & Privacy and click the General tab.

6 Click Require password <u>immediately</u> after sleep or screen saver begins.

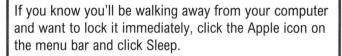

Did you know?

You can configure the Require password option in Step 6 to be enabled in a way other than 'immediately'. You may prefer 5 minutes, for instance, so that you have time to move the mouse to avoid entering a password if you're still at your desk when the screen saver is applied.

For your information

If you know you'll be walking away from your computer and want to lock it immediately, click the Apple icon on the menu bar and click Sleep.

Set energy-saving options ▶

Configure energy-saver settings

1 Open System Preferences>Energy Saver.

2 Use the sliders to set when the computer and the display sleep.

3 Configure other options as desired.

4 To cause your Mac to start up, wake or sleep at a specific time:

   a. Click Schedule.

   b. Configure preferences as desired.

   c. Click OK.

?

Did you know?

Computers use a lot of electricity. Configure all the computers in your home or office to go to sleep on a schedule and you'll probably see improvements in your electricity bill.

Part of maintaining a Mac is to let it rest (sleep, in Mac-speak) when you aren't using it. This is especially important for laptops running on battery power because it enhances battery life and lengthens the life of the battery overall. It also lets both desktops and laptops cool down, which is always good. Beyond the maintenance it provides your Mac, though, configuring energy-saving options can lower your electricity bill.

You can also configure energy-saving options so that your Mac wakes up and/or goes to sleep at a specific time that you set. For example, you may want your Mac to start up every day around 9am and go to sleep each day at 5pm. Alternatively, you may have a small Mac mini you use to listen to music at night, or to watch videos on during the evening's TV time. You could configure your Mac to come on at, say, 6pm each night and go to sleep automatically around midnight.

Finally, you can configure your Mac to start up again automatically if there's a power failure, allow the power button to put the Mac to sleep, wake the computer when someone on your local network wants access to it, or automatically restore if your Mac freezes. Hopefully your Mac won't freeze up very often, but it's an option if you need it.

There are times when your Mac just won't perform correctly. This will happen if the hard drive is corrupted, when an application freezes and you can't move your mouse or use the keyboard, or when a CD or DVD won't eject, for instance. It could be that your hard drive is full or that your laptop's battery is dead. Whatever the case, you need to know your troubleshooting options.

■ If the problem is due to a frozen application, see if you can 'force quit' it. Force Quit is an option available from the Apple menu on the menu bar. When you click Force Quit a window appears with the open applications listed. You can select the troublesome application and click Force Quit to close it.

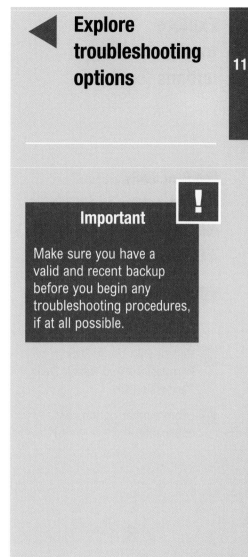

!

Important

Make sure you have a valid and recent backup before you begin any troubleshooting procedures, if at all possible.

■ If you suspect the hard drive is full (right-click Macintosh HD and click Get Info to be sure), delete large files, such as videos and TV shows, and then empty the Trash. You can search for Macintosh HD if you didn't place a shortcut for it in the Finder.

■ If the problem seems to be system-wide, try booting with a Safe boot and then rebooting normally after that. To Safe boot shut down the computer. Then hold down the Shift key on the keyboard and press the Power button. Hold down that key while the computer boots and until you see the login window or desktop.

■ Run Disk Utility, outlined next. This will verify the hard drive is healthy by checking the file system.

Explore troubleshooting options (cont.)

Use Disk Utility

1. Open Applications>Utilities.
2. Select Macintosh HD.
3. Click Show Details to watch Disk Utility's progress.
4. From the FirstAid tab, click Verify Disk; click Verify Disk again to proceed.
5. Repeat with Verify Disk Permissions and Repair Disk Permissions.
6. Explore other options as applicable.

■ If your Mac won't boot at all or freezes during the boot process and you don't have good backups, you can connect your Mac to another Mac computer with a FireWire cable and copy the files from it. Using what's called Target Disk Mode, you can transfer huge amounts of data very quickly or use Apple's Migration Assistant to transfer all your important files and settings from an existing Mac to a new one. To use this, connect the machines, boot the Mac that works and hold down the T key while pressing the Power button on the Mac that doesn't. Once booted, you should be able to access the files on the broken Mac.

■ If nothing else works, you can force the Mac to start from a bootable CD or DVD. You can then use that software to reinstall your system. To do this, insert the disk, restart the Mac and hold down the C key.

> !
> ## Important
> Apple offers a host of troubleshooting tips and techniques on its website. Visit *www.apple.com* and click Support to get started.

To reinstall Lion, you need to access Lion's built-in set of utilities in the Recovery HD. You also need to be connected to an Ethernet or Wi-Fi network. To get started, reboot your Mac and hold down the Command and R keys, and keep holding them until the Apple icon appears. With that done, look at the upper right corner of the screen and click the icon to display any available Wi-Fi networks and connect. Continue following the instructions provided to reinstall your Mac. If applicable, after the installation, download iPhoto, iMovie and GarageBand from the Mac App Store and reinstall your purchases. You can also copy data from your backups and perform any other required tasks.

Reinstall Lion

11

Jargon buster

AirDrop – This is a new Lion-only feature and enables two AirDrop-compatible Mac computers to share files wirelessly without setting up a network or joining one. You simply drag and drop files to the AirDrop interface and the user you select to share with can access them.

AirPort – Apple's 802.11b/802.11g standard for wireless networking. In pre-Lion Mac editions, AirPort was an option in System Preferences under Network. In Lion, that entry has been changed to Wi-Fi.

Alias – A shortcut to a file, folder or application on your Mac. Aliases use very little disk space and you can create any number of them for a single item. This means that you can put aliases for your most used items anywhere you like, including on the desktop or in folders or subfolders.

Apple menu – This is on the menu bar and is always available, regardless of what else is running. This menu gives you access to important system tools and information all the time, no matter what you're doing.

Application – A full-blown software package such as a word-processing suite or a movie-editing suite. Applications let you perform tasks, obtain media, send email and surf the Web, among other things. iWork is an application.

Apps – These are applications you get from the App Store. Apps can be just about anything, from a simple game that lets you fling birds into stacked objects (for only a few pounds) to a fully fledged program like Final Cut Pro X (which is much more expensive and complex).

Bluetooth – A technology for communicating wirelessly with devices such as computers, mobile phones, digital cameras, PDAs, printers and more. With a range of around 10 metres, Bluetooth poses no threat of interference and requires no licence or fee – you simply set up the devices to communicate and exchange data. Although individual devices have their own set-up routines, the procedures are broadly similar and OS X has a Bluetooth Setup Assistant to simplify the process.

Bookmark – Used in Safari, this is a shortcut to a web page you visit regularly. You can access bookmarks from the Bookmarks list or the Bookmarks bar, and you can create your own Bookmarks folders to organise what you amass.

Burning – The process of recording movies, music and data on to an optical disk such as a DVD or CD.

Cache – A special processor-only memory that remembers recent operations, thereby improving processing efficiency.

Compression – The technology used to make a file or folder take up less space on a hard drive or other medium. Compression is most commonly used when it's applied to data prior to sending it in an email, before uploading it to an FTP site or before archiving it.

Contextual menu – The menu you see when you Control + click. Generally you'll access these menus to get information about a file or folder, make an alias, duplicate the item, email it or burn it to disk.

Conversations – A new feature in Mail that allows you to view all your back-and-forth emails with a person (or a group of people) in one email window. When emails are grouped, you can easily locate all of them and view the progress of the conversation.

DHCP – Dynamic Host Configuration Protocol, essentially a method by which

a computer is assigned all it needs to join a network and get online without an administrator having to specify each component, such as a network address, individually.

DLS modem – A device that connects your Mac to your phone line to enable it to use a broadband Internet connection. Other technologies exist that are similar: cable modems, satellite modems, etc.

Dock – One of the most appealing features of OS X. The Dock runs across the bottom of the Mac desktop. The Dock offers at-a-glance access to applications, folders, the Trash and more.

Dock stacks – Stacks are groups of commonly used items you can access from a folder on the Dock. Your Mac comes with three built-in stacks: one for applications, one for documents and one for downloads. You can click any stack to see what's in there and click any item to open it.

Drives and volumes – A drive is a physical disk, the actual medium on which data is recorded. A volume is a logical drive, which is an area of a drive partitioned to look and behave just like a physical drive. You might, for example, have two, three or more partitions on a large drive and each will mount on the desktop and operate entirely independently of the others just like physical drives.

Encryption – A way to protect data from theft. When data is encrypted, a password must be entered to decrypt the data, which protects it from thieves and hackers. You do this using FileVault, an option in System Preferences, under Security.

Ethernet – A technology where data is sent from computer to computer via an Ethernet cable.

File type – A method to describe what a file is without having to open the file. Pictures are often jpegs and thus end in .jpg or .jpeg. Word files can be of various types, but are often in Rich Text Format (.rtf), a Word document (.doc), or even in Portable Document Format (.pdf). You can see what type of file you have from the Get Info window.

FileVault – A feature on your Mac that can be used to secure your Home folder. It is automatically encrypted and decrypted while you're using it.

Finder – Where you'll go to navigate to files, folders, pictures or applications stored on your Mac, and where you'll search for data you've recently created, imported from a camera, or saved on a connected external drive (such as a USB flash drive or SD card). So basically it's a place to locate your stuff. Beyond that, though, it's where you can perform system tasks like ejecting a CD or DVD, accessing networked computers, or moving or copying files and folders from one area of your Mac to another. The Finder is really the heart of the Mac's graphical user interface.

Firewall – A software mechanism for protecting the computer from Internet ills by assessing what's trying to come into your Mac. It does not let in data that is already known to be harmful.

Fonts (AKA typeface) – These are the alphanumeric and other characters displayed on the computer's screen (and reproduced on a printer) in a variety of shapes, sizes and styles. The size of a font character is measured in points (and known as the point size).

Gestures – If you have an external trackpad, or if you have a laptop with one built in, you can navigate the Mac's interface with hand movements called gestures. Mac Lion's new multi-touch gestures will make using your Mac easier. Common gestures are swipes, flicks, pinches and similar hand movements.

Graphical user interface – The menus, icons, lists, dialogue boxes, panes and so on that you use to do things, such as open and use applications, play music, watch videos, send email and save files. Before this type of interaction was available, users had to input computer commands like Print, etc. by typing them.

Hard drive – An area of your computer used to store data permanently.

HDMI – High Definition Multimedia Interface. This enables you to connect a superior display (monitor) for a better picture and viewing experience.

Home folder – This is your personal space on the Mac – it's where you put your files and folders. Your Home folder is the one with your name on it in the Finder and is represented by an icon of a house.

Hot Corner – An area of your Mac that you configure, so that when you move your mouse cursor to that corner of the screen, something happens. You might configure a Hot Corner to invoke a screen saver, for instance.

Hotspot – When you take your laptop to a public place such as a coffee shop, pub or hotel you may find that the establishment offers a Wi-Fi network that enables you to connect to the Internet for free. These types of networks are called 'hotspots' and are generally unsecured, meaning they do not require you to input a password.

iDisk – A feature in the Finder that you can use to set up MobileMe.

IMAP – Internet Message Access Protocol, used to access email messages from the Web.

ISP – Internet Service Provider. This is the organisation that provides you with Internet access, for a monthly fee.

Launchpad – A feature on your Mac that lets you organise, group and access apps.

Library – There are several Library folders. For the most part, the Library is managed and maintained by OS X and contains system-wide applications support files, fonts available to all users, data caches and other essentials that wise users (especially novices!) steer well clear of. There's also a Library folder in pre-Lion Home folders, which can contain fonts and certain other data accessible only to you.

Macintosh HD – This icon offers access to everything on your Mac's hard drive. Although you could use this option for finding data on your Mac, clicking your user name under Places is much easier.

Mail server – This is the server your ISP uses to send email and receive it: you'll have an incoming server and an outgoing server. You'll have to enter two mail server names (one for each) in Mail if prompted for the information. You'll need to ask your ISP for this information and type it exactly.

Media – A broad term used to represent just about anything you can view, read or listen to. On your computer this can be music, home videos, movies and audiobooks. It can also be pictures, radio shows, podcasts, TV shows, even playlists of your favourite songs.

Menu bar – A small, transparent bar that runs across the top of your Mac's screen. It's the bar with the Apple icon on it, the volume icon, and information about the network you're connected to, among other things. The menu bar also offers menus you can click to access the tools and features underneath.

Mission Control – This Mac Lion feature offers a bird's-eye view of everything open on your Mac. It's command central and brings together the Dashboard, Spaces, Expose and full-screen apps so that you can see everything at once.

MobileMe – A subscription service provided by Apple that lets you keep everything in sync on your Mac, PC, iPhone, iPad and iPod Touch. You have to pay for this service annually.

Phishing – The process of pretending to be a trustworthy entity (your bank, for instance) to acquire sensitive information such as account details, passwords and PIN numbers.

Playlists – These are lists you create to group media you feel should be grouped together. In iTunes, you can create a playlist of your favourite songs and then copy those songs to a CD, for instance, or you can create a playlist that contains songs you like to exercise to or drive with. You can also access playlists that are already created for you, such as Recently Added and Recently Played.

Podcast – A form of media that is often an informative lecture, news show, sermon or educational series offered free from colleges, news stations, churches and similar organisations. You can browse for free podcasts in the iTunes Store. If you find something you like, you can download a single podcast or subscribe to one to receive it on a schedule.

POP – Post Office Protocol, a system by which emails are retrieved from remote servers (that is, you connect to your ISP's POP server and collect your email).

Pop-ups – Uninvited and often insidious browser windows, usually smaller and hidden behind the window you've chosen to view and which pop up automatically to offer some dubious service when you visit a website. Where once pop-ups were a serious menace to your surfing enjoyment (dozens could be lurking behind legitimate windows), modern browsers such as Safari and Firefox have excellent pop-up blockers offering virtually 100 per cent success in keeping them at bay.

Protocol – A word used to describe the way two or more computers connect and exchange information. If both are operating with the same protocols, data exchange is possible.

RAM – Random Access Memory, a computer's memory chips. Used to hold data temporarily.

Rip – A term used to describe the action taken when you copy music that is on a CD you've purchased so that you can listen to that music on your Mac (without inserting the CD once it's been copied). You may opt to rip your entire CD collection so that you can listen to music without inserting CDs, to create your own CDs that contain mixes of your favourite songs, to share the music with networked computers, or to copy those songs to other devices you own, such as iPads or iPhones. Ripping a CD collection is the first place to start when populating iTunes (and your Mac) with music.

Router – A device that shares a broadband connection between several computers via an Ethernet or wireless (or both) network. Routers generally incorporate some sort of modem, such as cable, satellite or DSL. Routers can transfer data between two unlike networks too, such as the Internet and your home network.

RSS – Really Simple Syndication, a format for distributing frequently updated web content, such as news headlines, podcasts and blogs.

Screen savers – Graphical, moving images that engage to cover the screen and protect your computer from prying eyes after a specific period of idle time that you select. You can also require a password to disengage the screen saver, for more protection.

Secure Sockets Layer – Also called SSL, this is a secure authentication method for logging on to an email web server. Most of the time, this is your password.

SMTP – Simple Mail Transfer Protocol, the email-sending counterpart to POP. SMTP is used to configure your outgoing server in Mail.

Spotlight Search – Your Mac's personal search engine. Spotlight Search can help you locate your data. It's easy to use and there are Spotlight Search windows in lots of places, even in the Finder window and on the menu bar.

Trackpad – A device you use instead of (or alongside) a mouse to navigate and use your Mac.

Transition – A visual effect to link two scenes in a movie.

UNIX – OS X is a UNIX-based operating system comprising two layers: the underlying UNIX foundation that you don't ordinarily see and the highly intuitive graphic interface that you do. It's the graphical OS interface that lets you manipulate the computer with a mouse, menus, drop-down lists and dialogue boxes, among other things.

USB – Universal Serial Bus ports let you connect compatible devices, often mice, digital cameras, printers and scanners.

Utilities – A Mac folder that contains applications that help you perform system tasks, such as migrating computer settings and data from your old computer to your new one, getting information about your Mac (how much RAM or hard drive space you have, for instance) and fixing problems with your hard disk, including problems involving permissions for files, among other things. You won't use the utilities nearly as often as you use applications. In fact, you may never use them.

Volume – An attached drive such as the Mac's internal hard drive, a shared network drive, a pen drive and so on.

WEP – Wired Equivalent Privacy, an algorithm to secure a wireless network.

Widgets – Small apps available in Dashboard that you can use to quickly get information and perform common tasks. Default widgets include a calculator, a weather app, a calendar app and a clock. To access the Dashboard, and thus the widgets on it, press F12 on the keyboard.

Wi-Fi – A technology used to send data, get Internet access, print, connect computers and more without using Ethernet cable. It's not the same as cellular data; it's the technology you use in home and business networks that, once set up, is often free to the user.

Workgroup – A Windows term for a group of computers all belonging to the same network. Common workgroup names are MSHOME and WORKGROUP.

WPA – WiFi Protected Access, an algorithm to secure a wireless network.

Troubleshooting guide

Communicating with others via text and video

Maintenance and Security